Sophisticated Rebels

Some Books by H. Stuart Hughes

Oswald Spengler: A Critical Estimate (1952)

The United States and Italy (1953)

Consciousness and Society (1958)

History as Art and as Science (1964)

Prisoners of Hope (1983)

Between Commitment and Disillusion (1987)
   comprising
   The Obstructed Path (1968)
   The Sea Change (1975)

Sophisticated REBELS

THE POLITICAL CULTURE

OF EUROPEAN DISSENT

———— 1968–1987 ————

H. Stuart Hughes

HARVARD UNIVERSITY PRESS

CAMBRIDGE, MASSACHUSETTS

LONDON, ENGLAND

1988

Library of Congress Cataloging-in-Publication Data

Hughes, H. Stuart (Henry Stuart), 1916–
    Sophisticated rebels.

    (Studies in cultural history)
    Includes index.
    1. Europe—Politics and government—1945–
2. Dissenters—Europe.   I. Title.   II. Series.
D1058.H83 1988   940.55   88-527
ISBN 0-674-82130-0

*For Sandra and Kenneth
and David*

Contents

Preface

As a study of European dissent over the past two decades, *Sophisticated Rebels* is both personal in tone and selective in content. To my surprise, two of those who have already read it caught echoes of my very first book, *An Essay for Our Times,* published at precisely the half-century. Perhaps my surprise was misplaced: *Sophisticated Rebels* does indeed return after nearly four decades to the central concern of its remote predecessor, the outlook for dissent in an era of political reaction.

My title likewise echoes (with a drastic shift in emphasis) E. J. Hobsbawm's admirably provocative set of essays, *Primitive Rebels,* dating from a generation ago. My own work is similarly essayist in character; at the same time I have tried to link its individual chapters one to another by pursuing three guiding themes: nonviolence, limited goals, and skepticism about ideology, at least in the customary meaning of the term. Some readers may be puzzled at why I have chosen to deal with certain matters and omit others. I trust that most of my reasons will emerge from the context itself. I might add, however, that in writing of Pope John Paul II and of Jürgen Habermas, I have, in the first case, underlined the phenomenon of Catholics talking past each other, in the second case, concentrated on the philosopher engagé rather than on the theoretician whose thoughts are sometimes so abstruse as to baffle the uninitiated. I should also explain that the stress I put on the novels of Michel Tournier represents an effort to right an injustice: to date, Tournier's work has been insufficiently appreciated in my own country.

My closing date is June 1987—again for reasons which will emerge in due course. I have written the entire text (as is my invariable practice) in the past tense, to suggest its status as history rather than current events. Hence I have made no effort to update it as further events have unfolded during its passage toward publication. More particularly, in the case of Mikhail Gorbachev's reforms, I have thought it best to limit myself to the brief concluding paragraph of Chapter 7, which points toward grounds for hope in a still uncertain future while eschewing specific prediction.

Finally I should note that most of Chapter 2 was delivered as the Gottschalk Lecture in the Humanities at the University of Illinois at Chicago in October 1986, and a month earlier at Korea University in Seoul.

I n view of what I have already said, it may not be necessary to add that I have relied almost exclusively on my reading, my teaching, and my on-the-spot observations, without resort to the help of others. Three debts, however, I do want to acknowledge: to Pavils A. Zarins, of the Central Library, University of California, San Diego, for his persistence and inventiveness in tracking down the more elusive of my sources; to Aïda D. Donald and Ann Louise McLaughlin, of Harvard University Press, once again for their steady encouragement and meticulous, sensitive attention to detail. And, as always, I am immeasurably grateful to my wife, Judy, for her unique combination of editorial discernment, critical verve, and unwavering moral support.

H.S.H.

Sophisticated Rebels

ONE

"The Moral Equivalent of War"

"Political Culture": the expression has of late gained general currency. Though without precise definition, it seems to fit the task of appraising a set of disparate changes in Europe over the past two decades. Its meaning is sufficiently flexible to embrace religion, ethnic grievances, protests against tyranny, newly perceived social injustices, the quest for peace—even an imaginative literature not so much "engaged" as alert to shifts in public temper. In every case the innovators have stressed ethical concerns, some recent, some of long standing. A half-century ago Benedetto Croce wrote about the *vita morale:* he encouraged historians to view politics as the expression of wider aspirations extending over the full range of human culture. Croce's lesson can still guide us: what he called the ethico-political has never lost its relevance.

For the first two-thirds of the twentieth century it appeared practicable to subsume much of the ethico-political under the rubric of social thought. It proved possible to reach a rough consensus on a roster of leading thinkers and to trace the dominant themes they shared. By now that possibility has been foreclosed. Consensus has vanished. The criteria themselves of what constitutes a major statement about contemporary society have succumbed to bitter and often shrill debate. And this for good reason: the very notion of social thought was bound up with a situation in the practical world and a role for the intellectual within that world which we no longer recognize as our own. Battered by two world wars, forever collapsing and reviving, "bourgeois" society offered the subject matter for writers who enjoyed a privileged status within it, even when they proclaimed the goal of shaking it to its foundations. Little by little the society that lent itself to majestic generalizations has fragmented. With that process of fragmentation the intellectual in the old sense has become obsolete. A society of specialists—a society defined by rigorous and often mutually incomprehensible technical competences—is mirrored in an academic world of sharply demarcated "disciplines"; it has little use or room for the unattached, the free-floating, the *freischwebend* mind. We may take the death of Herbert Marcuse in 1979, and of Jean-Paul Sartre less than a year later, as symptomatic. Their successors are few.

Much of the foregoing may suggest a Marxian approach. And if it be Marxian to treat technological and economic "substructure" as preconditioning cultural "superstructure," so be it. But a self-styled Marxist would doubtless fail to accept so loose an allegiance; he would insist that a social class or alliance of classes be cast as protagonist of the story. The classes in question need not be proletarian in the traditional meaning of the term. Ever since the Frankfurt School's critique of the 1930s, "Western" Marxists have recognized that urban industrial workers have been losing (or shirking) their presumed historical function, and along with it the goal of "dictatorship." For the latter, Antonio Gramsci's concept of hegemony has furnished an acceptable substitute: with its emphasis more on persuasion than on force, and on cultural values along with economic power, hegemony conveys a modernized and reassuring ring. But is it what the struggles of the past twenty years have been about? Can one find any recognizable class that has been striving toward it? Have Turkish "guest workers," Welsh home-rulers, the stalwarts of Poland's Solidarity, Soviet dissidents, militant ecologists, feminists, and marchers for peace aimed at anything so heady and all-embracing? Obviously not. Hegemony will not serve as an ideological tent or umbrella. Nor will any other grand category. In trying to understand the multiple discontents of contemporary Europeans, one is obliged to proceed case by case.

And to pursue one's subject matter through the interstices of conventional formations: it lies somewhere between political parties and pressure groups, and between "high" and popular culture. Much of it fails to achieve coherent expression; we must learn from the garrulous and the inarticulate, from those who find it hard to put their thoughts on paper. "There are moments," a discerning Pole has declared, "when the unwritten values create the culture."[1]

In this inchoate constellation the supremely articulate peoples, the French and the British, shine less brightly than they did a generation or two ago. Observers who have tried to define the social evolution of those peoples during the 1970s have sounded puzzled; neither of their subjects was changing as markedly as the script demanded. In Britain there remained "a gulf between the proponents of the new culture and the older generation," in France, an "insular . . . debate" or series of debates, a self-concentration which "mattered less in the old days, when French culture and thought were globally supreme and radiated their own universality."[2] As the century entered its last quarter, innovation in political culture for the most part was springing up elsewhere—in Germany, in Eastern Europe, and along the Mediterranean.

In reckoning with such innovation, this book will move from country to country as the focus of concern shifts from one movement to another. In each case the most striking or characteristic manifestation has dictated the locale. Already a number of these manifestations are beginning to look like lost or near-lost causes. But their failure, possibly temporary, furnishes no excuse for not writing about them. As E. P.

3

Thompson reminds us, "casualties of history" are "valid in terms of their own experience"; still more, in "lost causes . . . we may discover insights into social evils which we have yet to cure."[3] Thompson was writing about an era of conservative resurgence two centuries ago; his reminder applies with equal force to the ascendancy of conservative government and values over the past two decades. In both cases those who thought or think *otherwise* deserve respectful attention. In our own time theirs have been the voices raised in protest against what conformists themselves have recognized as social evils: the manipulative routine of centralized, bureaucratic authority, whether in public or in private hands; the "massification" and soullessness of life in the sprawling "conurbations" that Europe's cities have become; the deadening of sensibility that has enabled the majority to screen from consciousness the impending nuclear peril.

The account begins in the spring of 1968. Two series of events—one in Paris and one in Prague—together mark the single clearest caesura in the history of Europe since 1945. So participants viewed them, and so they appear today. Though unrelated, they showed curious resemblances: both were brief, both almost bloodless, both utterly defeated. And in their psychological effects they were mutually reinforcing. Together they challenged the accepted wisdom about the post-Second World War social settlement. In East and West alike they broke through the prevailing assumption that populations would remain forever passive and inert: in the one case, bowed down by tyranny, in the other, lulled and gratified by the longest and most sustained experience of prosperity in nearly half a century. Almost without warning, in Paris as in Prague, dazzling hope flared up with breathless suddenness and fervor. In both cities that hope was extinguished. But the discontents that inspired it would not so quickly disappear. After 1968 the political culture of Europe could never return to what it had been before.

" The moral equivalent of war": William James's familiar expression acquired a new meaning in the month of May on the improvised barricades of the Parisian Left Bank. For the first time since the early years of the century a generation was coming of age without knowledge of major international conflict. By the melancholy timetable of the century's first half, the hour had struck for a third world war. Blessedly, no war came—at least in Europe. But young people, in Paris as elsewhere, were yearning for a fight; ignorant of actual violence, they cultivated its rhetoric. An age cohort swollen in numbers gloried in its own strength. Its very size had helped produce its grievances: overcrowded classrooms, too few professors, and the rigidities of a higher educational system designed for a smaller, an elite student population. Doubtless university youth has always found something to protest against. In the 1930s it was fascism and depression. But the young of that decade assumed that their "wretchedness . . . could not possibly last." The Second World War proved them right. The young of the 1960s saw "the wretchedness of affluence" stretching "endlessly before them."[4] In Paris above all, youth felt stifled. The bizarre blend of nationalist assertiveness and material satisfaction associated with General Charles de Gaulle's ten-year rule had engendered a smugness, a *suffisance,* almost without parallel.

It was surprising enough that a student insurrection should have gained significant working-class support. It was still more surprising that the alliance of the two by the end of May 1968 should have reduced the government to impotence in the French capital. What was perhaps most surprising of all was that once the authorities had regained their nerve, the insurrectionary movement should have collapsed in two weeks' time. This puzzling succession of happenings, which contemporaries diplomatically referred to as "the events of May," left behind two contrasting sets of memories.

The first was of euphoria. Participants have recalled an intoxicating sense of "transgression," of a breach in the established order, a "kind of awakening, of attention crystallized on things which passed for normal, habitual, institutionalized things, which suddenly lost their character as institutions." Nor did students alone occupy university buildings and swarm through the streets of the Left Bank; junior faculty and even a few senior professors accompanied and supported them. So did a handful of physicians and administrators. For once the barriers of speech and manners dividing students from workers seemed also to have been breached. Together fledgling intellectuals and sympathizers from the industrial suburbs groped for a new political language. At all-night meetings in lecture halls once hallowed by magisterial learning, weary, disheveled young men and women, haltingly or in torrents of verbiage, sought to define a future order that would abolish not merely economic exploitation but the pervasive psychic alienation weighing upon the impoverished and the privileged alike.[5]

The second set of memories mixed anger and irony. The doyen of France's liberal-conservative theorists, Raymond Aron, dismissed the revolt as sound and fury—a "vast charade" which reduced him to fury also. The indignation this "unreason" aroused, he freely confessed, exceeded anything he had previously experienced; the "disintegration" of academic procedures and standards, he explained, had swelled monstrously out of proportion to "the legitimate grievances" that had provoked it. The result was "psychodrama"—a "colossal release of suppressed feeling . . . It was . . . psychodrama rather than . . . real drama because of the absence of a revolutionary party"; because "everyone . . . indulged in role-playing" (including Aron, by his own admission cast as Alexis de Tocqueville). "The most striking thing about it was the verbal delirium, with no one killed."[6]

Diametrically opposed interpretations? Not quite. Apologists and critics could agree on the pivotal situation of a

Communist Party reluctant to endorse large-scale industrial strikes and rejecting any thought of armed confrontation with the government. They could also recognize, whether with regret or with the self-assured wisdom of experience, that the explosion of pent-up hatred had tried to do too many things at once; it had taken aim not only at the university system but at all the multiple establishments fettering the imaginative and the young. It had lacked clearly defined goals and a slogan readily grasped, a slogan on the model of Lenin's 1917 "peace and land." So it had been with the Revolution of 1848, the closest thing to a precursor of the events of May, on which those events shed retrospective light as an undertaking ill-conceived from the start. First had come a heartwarming moment of fraternity, then the chill of reality when the "party of order" reconstituted itself for a counteroffensive. And as had happened 120 years earlier, in a similarly spontaneous, incoherent fashion, the contagion had spread eastward from Paris—notably to the universities of Germany and Italy, with Britain, as before, only mildly infected. The yearning to refashion everything, everywhere, at one stroke (on this again, apologists and critics could agree) had diffused the effectiveness of revolutionary ardor and facilitated the triumph of its enemies.

A decade later a not-unsympathetic German commentator reached the bleak conclusion that the failure of the May insurrection—and more particularly the failure of French Communism to extend it full support—had "shattered . . . more than one . . . left-romantic illusion . . . Suddenly it became . . . apparent that the aggressive form of cultural criticism . . . was not to culminate in political action." The resulting shock recalled (and even perhaps surpassed) "the rude awakening experienced by a host of prominent European Marxists over the Moscow trials of the 30s."[7]

The writer might have added that within less than a year's time De Gaulle had departed from the scene.

7

In nearly every sense events in Prague in 1968 bulked larger than those in Paris. They lasted longer, seven months (January to August) as against one; they probed society more deeply; their leadership behaved more realistically and responsibly. In Prague mature, experienced figures took the lead. Students simply provided support and from time to time a goad to speedier and more thoroughgoing action. And the students in question thought and spoke very differently from their Parisian counterparts. "They had no desire to destroy their universities. They had no quarrel with the older generation . . . Instead of considering the university a microcosm of the society, they considered it . . . a club or pressure group within the society"—a group whose pressure needed to be deployed on behalf of freedom. Nor had they any quarrel with the bourgeoisie as such. "They had . . . the modesty and determination of . . . clear and limited aims."[8] To them, as to students throughout Eastern Europe, the anger of Western youth seemed nothing short of incomprehensible, the anger of the lucky, the pampered, people innocent of what a true struggle for fundamental liberty of the mind entailed.

The Czechoslovak attempt to institute "socialism with a human face" contrasted markedly with both its predecessor and its successor in the cycle (at twelve-year intervals) of national movements of resistance to Soviet control. As opposed to the fortnight of impassioned rebellion in 1956 in Budapest and its bloody suppression by Soviet tanks, what happened in Prague unrolled quietly, cautiously, with the deliberate design of avoiding provocative or inflammatory rhetoric. As opposed to the rise of Poland's Solidarity in 1980–81, liberalization in Czechoslovakia proceeded within the parameters of Communist rule and for the most part in channels specified by the reforming wing of the Communist Party. Yet despite their air of expert steersmanship, those at the helm never fully appreciated the implications of what they were doing, never understood that they were in over their heads. Nor did the Russians. Confusion in Moscow responded to confusion in Prague.

Ostensibly the Soviet Union had dominated Czechoslovakia for two decades—ever since the coup of 1948 that had brought multiparty rule to an end. In fact the "Muscovite" Communists' monopoly of power had begun to waver as early as 1966. The year following, at the Czech Union of Writers' congress, the opposition had spoken out boldly, bitterly, more particularly in condemnation of censorship. A rising novelist, Milan Kundera, had praised the democratic tradition of his country's interwar republic. The publication and immense popularity of Kundera's *The Joke* gave evidence, first, of a de facto relaxation of restrictions on publishing, second, of a widespread demand to hear and read the truth.

Hence the Soviet leadership had little reason for surprise at the course of events in Czechoslovakia after the choice in early 1968 of Alexander Dubček as Communist Party chief. Yet the evidence suggests bewilderment on the part of Leonid Brezhnev and his colleagues in the Kremlin. The Czechs were neither exploding nor breaking loose from the Warsaw Pact, as the Hungarians had done twelve years earlier; they were constantly protesting their loyalty to Moscow and its smaller allies; they were engaged in "creeping democratization" that made it difficult for the supervisory power to determine when or where to draw the line. The Soviet leaders lacked previous experience with this kind of evasive, soft-spoken dissidence. They waited until late July before deciding to prepare a plan for full-scale invasion. They waited another four weeks before determining to launch it. And they did so only when they became convinced, after a tense joint meeting at a Slovak border town, that their Czech counterparts had betrayed them and would not halt the process of reform. Brezhnev in particular seems to have opposed the

9

invasion plan almost to the end. "According to his own testi-
mony . . . , he had long defended Dubček as a 'good comrade' who could be relied upon to restore order."[9]

A characterization that would have struck contemporaries
as odd. During the early months of 1968 Dubček had established a reputation in the West as a stalwart of liberal democracy and a sure-footed political tactician. The reality was
more complex. Dubček never became all-powerful within
the Communist Party Presidium. He was neither able nor
apparently willing to govern with a firm hand. Decent,
modest, buoyed by a growing popularity, he little by little
began to radiate an unassuming version of charisma. But he
never fully transcended his background as an *apparatchik*
who had risen through the ranks of the party and still
thought in party organizational terms. On occasion he could
be "weak and indecisive"—a man groping his way in a situation very nearly as unfamiliar to him as to the Soviet Politburo itself.[10]

The drawbacks of Dubček's step-by-step approach
emerged with the publication in late June of the manifesto
entitled Two Thousand Words. Signed by more than sixty
men and women, including a number of leading scientists
and scholars, it called on the Czechoslovak people to awake
from the euphoria of the "Prague Spring." What had been
accomplished so far—notably in regard to freedom of speech
and of the press—received its commendation. What the document stressed, however, were the dangers ahead: from entrenched, old-line Communists capable of sabotaging the reform program; "from the possibility that foreign forces"
might "interfere" with Czechoslovak internal development.
In countering these perils, Two Thousand Words urged popular pressure for continued and more profound change.
Instead of waiting for action from above, ordinary citizens
should "display . . . personal initiative and determination."
They should launch "resolutions, demonstrations, . . .
strikes, and boycotts."

10

Although Two Thousand Words recognized the impossibility of conducting "some sort of democratic revival without the Communists or . . . against them," it bluntly denied that they deserved any "gratitude." Not so Alexander Dubček. In a television and radio address which indirectly responded to it three weeks later, he defended his party's unique ability to "comprehend and understand the interests, desires and needs of . . . working people." He voiced his confidence that the Czechoslovak Communist Party would pass the "historic test" of leading the country toward a form of socialism "rooted in the soil" and corresponding to "national conditions and . . . traditions." He concluded with the fatherly admonition that democracy was "also a conscious civic discipline" requiring "statesmanlike wisdom of all citizens."[11]

To be sure, Dubček was speaking under severe constraints. He was primarily replying to criticism directed against him by the leadership of his presumed allies in the Warsaw Pact. Yet it is difficult to escape the conclusion that he sidestepped, by a resort to reassuring phrases, the vexing questions raised in Two Thousand Words; he never closed the gap between loyalty to his party and sympathy for his people's democratic aspirations. By the same token, he failed to exploit the wave of sympathy flowing toward Czechoslovakia from Italy. After all, the Italian Communists, like himself, were moving step by step toward "socialism with a human face." Still more, the solidarity they expressed with their counterparts in Prague marked a further (and crucial) stage in their evolution toward democracy and rupture with Moscow. As the summer of 1968 wore on, like Czechoslovakia itself, Dubček was hovering in a twilight zone in which the basics were yet to be defined.

A similar uncertainty clouded the prospects for the extraordinary congress of the Communist Party scheduled for September (and of course aborted by the invasion). Clearly the roster of delegates and of candidates for election to the

Central Committee indicated a turnover of political personnel unprecedented in the history of Communist regimes. But to the key question of whether the congress would opt for "a completely open and competitive . . . system" or for maintaining a single party's "continued leadership . . . within a system of limited pluralism," the preparatory documents gave no unequivocal answer. All one can say with assurance is that the reformers among the Communist leadership, including those rated more progressive than Dubček, had not yet declared themselves prepared to go beyond piecemeal democratization to "a fully pluralist society."[12]

Moreover, Dubček and his colleagues "underestimated or ignored the possibility of military intervention"; apparently they dismissed it as unlikely. When it came, they found their country defenseless. Czechoslovakia's geographical location, virtually surrounded, as it was, by other Warsaw Pact countries, made armed resistance impracticable. The most its leaders could manage was a courageous, dignified refusal to serve as Soviet stooges, backed up by nearly universal passive resistance on the part of the civilian population, and a dogged and ultimately futile effort to salvage the essentials of reform. As what was euphemistically termed "normalization" month by month eroded Czechoslovakia's fragile proto-democracy, it became apparent that the brave hope of "reconciling the irreconcilable" had vanished.[13]

Illusion in Prague echoed illusion in Paris. Where the exuberant French insurrectionists had looked in vain to Communism as a revolutionary force, the sober Czech reformers had counted on Soviet tolerance for liberal measures. Both had failed to appreciate that Moscow would countenance neither revolution nor democratization, that Brezhnev was settling for the status quo—in this respect much like De Gaulle's two conservative successors, Georges Pompidou and Valéry Giscard d'Estaing. It was a bitter truth which

Russia's dissidents understood better than independent spirits who lived farther removed from the center of Communist strength; of the former, only a handful reckoned on bringing about fundamental change with the confines of the Soviet system.

In France and in Czechoslovakia alike the basic miscalculation derived from an underestimate of established power structures. Armies, police forces, and self-perpetuating oligarchies held the key. They might temporarily be thrown off balance, but once they had grasped what an unprecedented situation required, they knew how to deal with it quickly, efficiently, bloodlessly. Whether such power structures were indigenous or foreign mattered little to the ultimate outcome.

It is impossible to determine how much of the above-mentioned realities rose to conscious awareness in the minds of Europe's dissidents. What is incontrovertible is that, after 1968, protest took on a variety of novel guises, working for the most part with quiet tenacity on the margin or periphery rather than at the center of established power. In some cases, as with the German Greens, disabused veterans of student unrest turned to nonviolent action on behalf of new causes their fellow citizens cared little about. In other cases, as with movements for the reassertion of historic cultures, it was untried local spokesmen who sought to bring to public attention centuries-old injustices whose very existence the dominant majority scarcely suspected. We may call both types of protest "sophisticated"—sophisticated in the sense of recognizing realistic limits and frequently defying conventional classification as right or left.[14]

A further and final novelty: to those who scorned to think in stale, weary categories, the division of Europe into a Communist East and a democratic, capitalist West seemed a crueler and crueler anomaly. On both sides of the divide there mounted a longing to reunite European culture. Naturally the cry rang out more insistently from the East, and

13

perhaps most poignantly from writers driven into exile. An itinerant Pole could surmise that his and comparably tormented nations might "become Europe's new center of experience," where "future forms of community life" were being born, "forms that at some point" the West would need. Milan Kundera could remind his French and German and British readers that with the eclipse of Poland and his own Czechoslovakia, Western culture was threatened with the loss of an integral, a precious part of its heritage.[15] Stubbornly, passionately, Kundera and his like refused to give up the hope that some day Europe would again be one.

TWO

The Parisian Scene:
The Return of the Novel

"A structure cannot descend into the streets." The quip attributed to the young Parisian insurgents of May 1968 epitomizes the irony in the triumph two years earlier of the intellectual current loosely termed structuralism. In 1966 *The Order of Things,* Michel Foucault's reflection on cultural history, had appeared close together with Jacques Lacan's collected psychoanalytic *Écrits.* Their publication had suggested that "a distinctive 'moment' had been reached in contemporary French thought, the first such" since the breakthrough of Sartrean existentialism two decades earlier.[1]

The irony lay in the fact that, aside from a certain diffused rebelliousness, structuralism could furnish the militant students no ideological rationale or buttressing. However its practitioners might sympathize with the insurgents' aims, what they taught bore little on insurgency itself. On the contrary, their writings conveyed a basic denial of ideology. They offered a substitute—a surrogate infatuation—for the Marxist allegiance of Parisian intellectuals that by the mid-1960s was already wavering. They inherited "the same ambition for total, systematic understanding," and a "deep relationship, both contrary and homogeneous," to it. The old dream persisted, but "'deideologized' and freed from the naïvetés of commitment and of the meaning of history."[2]

Beyond its lack of revolutionary relevance, structuralism

15

impinged only tangentially on political culture. Linguistics, the science of "signs": these were the concerns that gave a semblance of unity to an inordinately diverse set of writers. Moreover, their obsession with language set up an almost insuperable barrier for the average reader. The structuralists scorned the traditional French virtue of clarity. It was not that they wrote badly out of sloppiness or ignorance. It was rather that they cast their work consciously and defiantly in a dense, elliptical style, replete with long, clotted sentences, neologisms, and wordplay. At its best, as in the case of Roland Barthes, semiologist and literary critic, the writing exhaled a gently teasing charm. At its most extreme, as with the poststructuralist Jacques Derrida, it led the irreverent reader to suspect that the author might have his tongue in his cheek, might be addressing himself to an initiated few who knew whether and when to take him at his word.

Derrida wrote so little of the "real world" that we may safely exclude him from our account. The same holds for two others customarily listed among a canonical six, though for quite different reasons. By 1968 Louis Althusser, the pontiff of structural Marxism, was assuming the air of a belated survivor from the ideological era. By the same date Claude Lévi-Strauss, secure at the pinnacle of his profession of anthropology, had won an international reputation impervious to current fads; moreover, he wrote with elegance and (most of the time) with lucidity. This process of elimination leaves us with the trio Barthes, Foucault, Lacan, all three of whom died between 1980 and 1984. Their passing suggested that structuralism's decade and a half of dominance might have passed with them. It also offered a base point for a provisional assessment of what, if any, inspiration or guidance they bequeathed to new forms of political culture.

At first glance their legacy may strike us as almost wholly negative. Political culture stems from historical roots. The trio in question dealt in tightly ordered cross sections of thought and conduct rather than free-flowing continuities,

16

and subscribed to positivist rather than historicist epistemo-
logical assumptions. Of the three, Foucault alone concerned
himself with history. But the model of the past he prescribed
jarred conventional categories by its "archaeological" cast. It
traced no uninterrupted process; it delineated the human sciences as a series of layers called epistemes, closed off one from
another and lasting perhaps a century and a half. That Foucault dated the onset of the current one around 1950 con-
signed to irrelevance nearly all precedent and example from
the episteme immediately preceding.

Even more, he, in common with his peers, shared "a way
of thinking opposed to individualism, or even to humanism," in which "intentional human agency" played a
"reduced role," a thought pattern of "dissolution, of disbe-
lief in the ego." This antisubjectivist bent often left struc-
turalist accounts devoid of actors or speakers. Abstractions
served instead—or possibly a "complex series of relations
with no precise referents."[3]

Two disparate examples give tangible evidence of the
inhumanity, even cruelty, of such a procedure. The first is
Lacan's clinical method. The self-styled apostle of a return to
Freud, sworn foe of the American-based ego psychologists
whom he accused of betraying the founder, Jacques Lacan
practiced on his analysands a technique close to hysteria, "in
a theatrical mold." Histrionic in his own behavior, he imposed surprise and shock on those who sought his help. The
"short session" epitomized the process. Just when the analy-
sand thought he was getting into material of crucial signifi-
cance to self-understanding, Lacan would abruptly stand up
and declare the session "over, finished, done with." The effect "was like a rude awakening, like being torn out of a
dream by a loud alarm. (One person likened it to *coitus in-
terruptus*.) . . . There was something of the horror of death in
the short sessions, . . . whose time could not be known in
advance, whose time was not counted by the ticks of a
clock." With Lacan death stood mercilessly waiting in the

wings. "He placed his work in direct opposition to the ideological bias toward life, toward being, toward the flowing of an essential humanity."[4]

The second example is drawn from the celebrated conclusion to Foucault's *The Order of Things*. In it he pronounced man (in the sense understood by humanists) a recent "invention," a characteristic intellectual product of the "modern" episteme, which had begun around 1800 and had recently ended. By the same token, Foucault surmised, man could disappear. One might wager that he would eventually "be erased, like a face drawn in sand at the edge of the sea."[5]

After these bleak words, what can we place on the positive side of the ledger? What can we find to pit against the denigration of the individual and the humane, values by which the new political-cultural movements set great store? Initially a bracing dose of "demystification." The term signified the exposure of humbug, the impudent shout that the emperor was parading naked, already familiar from the work of Marx and Freud. What the Parisian structuralists added were probes for deception concealed in minutiae, subliminal messages hidden in ostensibly value-free images and expressions. Here the linguistic emphasis took on a subversive political relevance. More particularly in the writings of Barthes—the most "human" of the three, who celebrated pleasure in a text and ultimately learned to enjoy his own existence—we can trace an abiding obsession with demasking the mythical. Through constant and disconcerting shifts of focus over two decades, we can trace an arc of continuity.[6] Already in 1957, in *Mythologies,* his first influential book, Barthes had explained how the constricting verbal categories of the bourgeoisie constituted "a prohibition for man against inventing himself." Twenty years later, in his inaugural lecture as professor at the Collège de France, he was still warning against the coercive power of language. People failed to appreciate this coercion, he argued, because they forgot that all language involved "classification" and that all classification was "oppressive."

Foucault and Lacan agreed. For them as well, ideology—a peculiarly insidious manifestation of the power of language—ranked as a grandiose mystification obscuring the realities of dominion. Power, they maintained, lurked everywhere, even among the forces of liberation which were trying to counteract it. Those who claimed to have released what had been "crushed" were themselves engaged in crushing elsewhere.[7] The reminder suggested a second aspect of structuralism that dissident movements might find congenial.

The reverse of the admonition about power's mystifying effect as channeled through language was a sympathetic concern for the authentically marginal. It peeped through Barthes' ripe reflection on literature as "desacralized, . . . *no longer protected,*" freed from the conventional "model of the human" in "a moment of gentle apocalypse." It was implicit in Lacan's self-definition as a psychoanalyst who jettisoned professional routines and ferreted out the bizarre wherever he could scent it. It surfaced when Foucault wrote of the still "unthought," the second self, the "twin," linked to ordinary humankind "in an unavoidable duality."[8] Indeed, Foucault's absorption with the phenomena of madness and incarceration epitomized at their sharpest a shared effort to vindicate the claims of those whom society had cast out or reduced to invisibility.

The new forms of political culture were invariably marginal in one or another sense. Sometimes, as in the case of foreign workers, the protagonists perceived themselves, and were perceived by others, as derelicts. More often, as with movements of cultural reassertion, the marginality derived from a conscious choice tinged with pride. In either case, writers such as Barthes or Foucault or Lacan had anticipated what was coming or was already in the air. They had helped to pry apart established patterns of language and thought, to open crevices through which what had gone unnoticed could at last become visible.

Not all the veterans of the Events of May managed to traverse the ordeal with such equanimity. Just under a decade later, Parisians rushed to buy the effusions of two repentant and still youthful insurrectionists: André Glucksmann's *The Master Thinkers* and Bernard-Henri Lévy's *Barbarism with a Human Face* (the latter title a snide reevocation of Dubček's ill-fated venture in Prague). These "new philosophers," as the press pretentiously labeled them, seemed to take ferocious joy in breast-beating and repudiation of their own past. With the fevered, overblown, repetitive rhetoric of rage, they denounced the horror they had discovered in socialism. Much of what they were now detailing, they admitted, had been familiar for decades. But it had required the Dante of their time, the contemporary guide through the inferno, Alexander Solzhenitsyn, to drive the message home. In this respect Glucksmann and Lévy faithfully mirrored their readers' mentalities. It was symptomatic of France's lingering cultural provincialism that only with the publication of *The Gulag Archipelago* in the early 1970s did its complacent intellectuals of the Left awake from their dogmatic slumbers.

Had Glucksmann and Lévy limited themselves to an exposé of Soviet "barbarism," the critical reader might have questioned their originality but not their sanity. When, however, the one pointed an accusing finger at German nineteenth-century philosophers as the "master thinkers" who had "erected the mental apparatus . . . indispensable for launching the grand final solutions of the twentieth century," and the other lumped together without discrimination all forms of socialist theory and practice as variants on Soviet-style Marxism, one might at the very least suspect them of irresponsible exaggeration. And also of extravagant mental gymnastics: American fliers dropping bombs on Cambodia would have been astounded to learn that they were engaged in acting out an "unproclaimed Hegelianism."[9]

This much can be said for Glucksmann and Lévy: they evenhandedly discerned in Western behavior the warning signals of what had already occurred in the East. For them, as for Barthes and Foucault, the realities of naked power predominated everywhere. The notion of legitimacy had collapsed; over the bent backs of docile populations, the authorities could perpetrate with impunity whatever abominations took their fancy. In a world Lévy termed "a disaster," with humanity "an aborted species," barbarism, totalitarian rule, figured as the norm. For the intellectual there remained only the "noble" stance of stoic pessimism, of stubborn fidelity to "the virtues of an atheist spiritualism."[10]

By the end of the 1970s the "new philosophers" were finding successors in a "new Right." Neoconservatism, in France, as in Britain and the United States, had become fashionable. But by this time the French version at least had lost its point. From an extra-Parisian perspective, it already appeared dated.

Again and again over the previous quarter-century, French and foreign observers alike had heralded an opening up or out, an escape from cultural claustrophobia.[11] This feat the strenuous young conservatives clearly had not accomplished. Nor had the structuralists and their successors. Although they had established a stern hegemony over academic literary criticism, they had failed to do the same for the "discourse" (to use their own term) of political culture.

The opening, when it occurred, came from an unexpected quarter. It came in a return of the novel. By the late 1960s the demise of French narrative fiction seemed a foregone conclusion. The novel had succumbed to a double assault. First a set of fastidious literary craftsmen (once again labeled "new") such as Alain Robbe-Grillet and Nathalie Sarraute had jettisoned both plot and character delineation. Subsequently the critics, structural or post-, had taken to lecturing novelists on how to go about their labors, subjecting them to unremitting dissection, along with the arrogant and scarcely veiled claim that their own ranked as a loftier form of literary endeavor. No wonder younger novelists complained of a writing block imposed by intellectual "terror"!

On this depressing landscape there erupted a major figure who dared to write a "real story." When in 1970 he published his eccentric and highly personal elaboration on Goethe's ballad "The Erl-King," Michel Tournier, already in his mid-forties, was just beginning to reach a belated literary prominence. Three years before, with *Friday,* he had won a *succès d'estime*. He had delighted his readers with a retelling of the Robinson Crusoe story—a reworking in which the savage and docile "man Friday" took over from his master the role of guide or "midwife" in exploratory ventures beyond conventional civilization into the "unheard-of" and the "unforeseeable."[12] Already Tournier was reaching for the "elsewhere" that would become his hallmark.

But it was his Erl-King that made his fame, that gained him a readership combining breadth and discrimination. Into it he had gathered the fragments of his own life that had touched him most deeply—and a decade and a half of reflection and painful, disheartening literary composition. The novel took the form of both personal metamorphosis and a picaresque journey ever farther into Germany. To its protagonist, an ungainly, half-blind colossus of a man, with big hands, a diminutive penis, and a voracious appetite for raw meat, the military mobilization of 1939 brought release from a mediocre existence and with it a sense of vibrating at last to the pulse of great events. Unlike the run of Frenchmen, he shrugged off national defeat and the captivity that followed. He learned to love the country and the people that held him in thrall; he resolved never to return to the land of his birth.

22

And as he progressed deeper and deeper into the landscape of his dreams, as he labored in peat bogs along the Baltic and served as assistant forester at the vast hunting preserve of the half-sinister, half-comic "ogre" Hermann Goering, he began to see in himself the reincarnation of a primeval German king—an image modeled on a two-thousand-year-old corpse dug up from the peat in a state of near-perfect preservation.

The end found him, appropriately enough, in East Prussia, at the farthest outpost of German culture and the first to be overwhelmed by the Red Army, now himself metamorphosed into a species of ogre, as he roved the countryside on horseback, kidnapping preadolescent "Nordic" boys for enrollment in a Nazi elite training school. Yet this reenactment of Goethe's ballad, this assumption of the role of boy-snatcher, alike fearsome and seductive, conveyed a double meaning. The finale brought the slaughter of the young Nordics, vainly defending their fortress school against the Soviet invaders, and, in counterpoint with it, the equally vain attempt on the part of the Erl-King to bear to safety on his shoulders an alien child, an emaciated Jewish death-camp survivor whom he had carried off during one of his forays and hidden in that very fortress. The novel closed with the swallowing-up of the two—the boy and his "Steed of Israel"—by "the soft and treacherous soil of the moor" on which they had taken refuge.[13]

These last lines suggested that the title chosen for the English translation, *The Ogre,* gave only a partial and misleading glimpse into a protagonist whom Tournier called a "poor giant . . . hungry for tenderness, near-sighted and visionary, constantly joining his enormous hands together like a cradle for sheltering some little child." They also evoked the moral universe, steeped in ambiguity, of a writer who reckoned as the "three essential attributes" of intelligence the apparently incompatible qualities of "subtlety, pomp, and fun."[14]

Certain biographical peculiarities may help to explain the unique stance "elsewhere" at which Tournier eventually arrived. Born a Parisian in 1924, he came to detest his birthplace; as a mature man he preferred to live in a quasi-rural setting, south of the city, venturing infrequently into a capital made unlivable by a "stupid" sacrifice of man to automobile. Four years of Catholic schooling marked him for life: his vocabulary, his turns of phrase, derived from the tradition of the Church and meditation on the Bible. Yet his allegiance to the faith, if such it could be called, bore the same stamp of the idiosyncratic as his other affective ties. He could admire in ritual pomp "the need for jubilation" he shared with the poor and the uneducated. His soul recoiled from the "horror of the flesh" and of sexuality that had set the grisly symbol of the crucifix "at the center of Catholic worship." Tournier's notion of Christianity was suffused with tenderness coupled to a gentle eroticism.[15] It found expression in one of his later novels, which retold the story of the homage of the three Magi to the newborn Jesus, and of a fourth (of his own invention) who arrived too late to behold the little savior but whose life became transformed into one of humble sacrifice by what he subsequently pieced together of the master's teaching.[16]

Above and beyond every other influence on Tournier's formative years stood the omnipresence of German culture. With both parents specialists in *Germanistik,* he grew up bilingual. So too had Jean-Paul Sartre, but in Sartre's later life this accomplishment, rare among the French, had gone little beyond granting him easy access to the treasure trove of German philosophy. Bilingualism went far deeper for Tournier; he nourished a passion for things German. From boyhood stays in Freiburg at a student lodging run by nuns and joyous expeditions into the Black Forest close by he acquired an abiding attachment to a countryside he found neat, ordered, reassuring. He also watched with fascination the growing military power of the Reich, and more particularly how boys of his own age were systematically enrolled in Nazi formations, and still more, how "the new German regime fixed its axis" on young people like himself. Yet neither he nor his parents succumbed to Hitler's rhetoric. In common with so many German Catholics, they held it at arm's length, secessionists without militancy. When a few years later the victors occupied their country, the Tournier family stood apart from the unsavory ranks of the collaborationists. They had already been "vaccinated against Nazi seduction."[17]

So Tournier, too young for military service, witnessed the occupation as an enthralled bystander. With the war's end his first thought was to return to Germany. Circumventing one bureaucratic hurdle after another, he succeeded in remaining there for four years. Of his life in the delightful university town of Tübingen (a Freiburg on a smaller scale), he recalled that if he ever had "known the intoxication of being young," it was unquestionably then. Confined, as previously, to the hilly, picture postcard southwest, he pored over maps and books about the Soviet-controlled northeast, of whose flat, misty, "metaphysical" landscapes he wrote with a curious nostalgia for a dreamland he had never seen.[18] Simultaneously he was discovering the agony of the East Prussians' winter flight from the Red Army. (He was later to shock his countrymen by referring to their own exodus of 1940 as "in comparison . . . an embarkation for Cythera.")[19] Evidently his Erl-King was already haunting him, as he began to gather material for his greatest novel.

Ostensibly, however, like Sartre or Raymond Aron before him, he was studying philosophy. This was what young Frenchmen were supposed to do in Germany—and in Tournier's case with obsessive rigor. But when it came time for his examinations back home in France, he failed them. His academic prospects now blighted, he took refuge in translating and working for the radio. It was almost despite himself that he eventually found his "situation" as a storyteller. Still these stories had a philosophical cast—sometimes to excess. An abiding self-definition as a philosopher joined his loathing for Paris, his infatuation with Germany, and his ambiguous attitude toward the Church among the defining features of a childhood and youth that were forever slipping away from preestablished categories.

In the end he settled (another Robinson Crusoe or Candide!) for solitude and total independence quite literally in his own garden. A "growing solitude," he once wrote, was "the most pernicious wound of contemporary Western man." Yet he preferred it to the alternative—a life of spurious sociability. "Works of art," he added, were "desert fruit" blooming "only in arid soil. Lord, give no ear to my supplications, and if by any chance I some day approach the oasis of a friendly heart in a welcoming body, send me back with kicks in the ass to my familiar steppes where a dry and icy wind blows."[20]

Earlier, Tournier's slow trek into literature had cut him off from the coteries of Paris. Subsequently he remained aloof by choice. Still, to add a final twist of ambiguity, despite the depth of his feeling for Germany, he took quiet pride in his status as a *French* writer (by which he meant a virtuoso of the language, not necessarily French by birth or nationality).[21] He took pride in the purity and limpidness of his style. Through that very style, as through the accessibility of his storytelling, he directed a standing rebuke to the purveyors of the faddish, the contorted, and the obscure who had so notably maltreated their common tongue.

Thus when election to the Académie Goncourt catapulted him into the Parisian literary establishment, Tournier continued to view himself as a chance arrival from elsewhere. He continued to protest against the frantic attempts of writers who had grown up within that establishment to "knock down" the inherited structure of the novel. His own aim sounded more modest—deceptively so: "to create something new while lending it an air of the déjà vu, . . . to slip . . . into a form as traditional . . . and reassuring as possible, matter having none of these qualities." This definition of his craft led him to respect the "concrete" and "savory" prose, steeped in life itself, of the great realist writers. It also (and in only apparent contradiction) led him to discern something in common between his work and the photographic precision of the Surrealist painters. It led him to take, as "encouragement and . . . incomparable model," Bach's "Art of the Fugue," whose "human and cosmic" content had become "all the richer, all the more moving," through the "pitiless . . . formal constraint" to which the composer had subjected it.[22]

What was this new material that Tournier fitted into his meticulously constructed frameworks? Where can one locate the center of his moral universe? By his own account in "inversion," in transformations into opposites. No wonder that his readers found his public stance bewildering. On the one hand, he seemed an archconservative, possibly a covert admirer of fascism, who could casually speak of the "beauty of violence and war." On the other, he directed his verbal violence at warmongers, past and present; he stigmatized the "absolute pessimism . . . characteristic of the ideology of the Right" as leading "logically to extermination camps and crematoria"; he marveled at the great German thinkers of Jewish origin whom he called the "pillars of modern Western civilization";[23] he traced his Erl-King's step-by-step progress toward giving up his life to save a Jewish child.

In the process of pitting one value against its opposite, the humane, the tender predominated at the end. And this was for a reason that only close reading between the lines would make apparent. For Tournier the events which gripped the attention of the public were epiphenomenal. Below (or above?) them lay affective phenomena with the power to transform, transmute, transfigure the world. Take the matter of sexuality. The homoerotic undercurrent was there for all to see, and with it both an endorsement of the flesh and a spirited defense of people's right to indulge in any form of "perversion" which caught their fancy. For Tournier himself, the twelve-year-old boy, just short of the "disaster" of puberty, ranked as creation's "masterpiece." But—and on this score he left no room for doubt—unbounded admiration could dispense with genital contact. Indeed such contact debased it by reducing it to the banality of everyday. The primary value resided not in sexuality but in *attachment* (and here Tournier echoed what Britain's psychoanalysts were already saying). It was immaterial whether the conventional labeled such an attachment homo- or hetero-. For his part Tournier welcomed the blurring of the line between the sexes that he detected in contemporary society; he detested "every accentuation of virility and femininity." He wrote of strong women and of tender men.[24]

Hence it followed logically that along with his celebration of nongenital love went a claim on behalf of his fellow males to a "maternal vocation." He found its epitome in what he named *"phorie"*: the act, the practice, of forcefully carrying off the object of one's love and then, almost against one's will, witnessing the transformation of that act into humble sacrifice. (It was doubtless with the author's consent that a picture of Saint Christopher bearing the infant Jesus figured on the cover of his Erl-King.) Beyond the clichés of "perversity" as against "mature" erotic fulfillment, Tournier discovered his supreme joy in carrying, in sheltering a child. For twenty years he relieved his bachelor loneliness by bringing up a godson in his own house. An eternal, if world-weary, child himself, he found in the very young his measure of what truly mattered. His aspiration to write "for everyone" notably embraced writing for children, which he did with relish. The best writers, he maintained, were those whom children could readily understand. "In truth," he summed up his hard-won wisdom, "the little one" was "always right."[25]

Milan Kundera, five years younger than Tournier, also wrote for everyone. He too composed his novels with a blend of fantasy and narrative precision. And he would have agreed in listing fun among the essential attributes of intelligence. But if Tournier's humor was elusive and laced with the sinister, Kundera's was out in the open, bordering on the belly-laugh. Along with it went a pervasive, utterly "normal" curiosity about sex. All of which is to say that Kundera was the simpler writer.

Tournier was a Frenchman by birth rather than choice. Kundera became a resident of France by *force majeure*. Moravian-born and the son of a talented pianist, as a university student he had gone through a Communist phase during the heady years of Czechoslovakia's short-lived near-democracy from 1945 to 1948. Cured of that infatuation, he had cultivated jazz music, the cinema, and, eventually, literature. When the publication of his first novel, *The Joke,* hoisted him to fame with the luminaries of the Prague Spring, it also made him a man over whom old-line Communists kept close watch. Along with Dubček and "liberals" of all shades, he lost his job in the reaction that followed. After seven years of a hounded existence, he left for France in 1975.

Denied publication in his own country, he continued to write in Czech; among the expanding circles of his readers, nearly all knew his stories only in translation. In common with Tournier, he resisted assimilation to the Parisian literary set. He nourished few illusions about it; France, he declared, "suffering from the lack of great historic events," reveled "in radical ideological postures." Yet it had become his "real homeland"; his stay there was "final"; he refrained from calling himself an émigré. The émigré lived in the hope of return to his native land. For Kundera and his like, such hope had been foreclosed; they were condemned to finish their days in a "tunnel . . . without end."[26]

Tournier had fastened on his German experience as the fulcrum of his writing. For Kundera it was the fate of the Czechs throughout history, recent and remote. In 1618 they had resisted foreign domination—and lost. In 1938, 1948, 1968, they had "opted for caution"—and again lost. "Should they have shown more courage . . . ?" one of Kundera's

29

characters asked himself in anguish. "What should they have done?" The speaker did not know; nor, apparently, did Kundera. The novelist remained haunted by the memory of hearing on the radio a "quavering voice," broken by "awful . . . pauses," as of a man gasping for air, the voice of Dubček reporting on futile "negotiations" in Moscow, the voice of a humiliated leader addressing "his humiliated nation." As another character in the same novel put it: after the first shock was over, "she realized that she belonged among the weak, in the camp of the weak, in the country of the weak, and that she had to be faithful to them precisely because they were weak and gasped for breath in the middle of sentences."[27]

But how was one to keep faith? For all his hesitations, Kundera offered two suggestions, both deriving from bitter self-knowledge. The first was a warning. With his own past in mind, Kundera alerted his readers to the "terrible" fanaticism of youth: "a stage trod by children in . . . fancy costumes mouthing speeches they've memorized . . . but only half understand." From novel to novel he shifted the metaphor with which he conveyed youth's passionate longing for single-minded social harmony. In one it took the form of *"an idyll, for all"*—"a garden" where "nightingales" sang, and "every man" was "a note in a magnificent . . . fugue." Or it might be visualized as angels dancing in a ring, magical, innocent. (Yet woe betide the true innocent who dared to slip away from the closed security of the circle; for him there was no return! So had it been with the author himself: "Like a meteorite broken loose from a planet," he had spun off and had been "falling ever since.") In a subsequent novel, the ring had changed into a "Grand March . . . , the splendid march on the road to brotherhood, equality, justice, happiness."[28] By that time (the mid-1980s) the metaphor had become immaterial. The thought, the warning, the pledge of fidelity to countrymen languishing in oppression back home, had by now taken their place as dependable features of Kundera's writing.

"History," he had concluded, was "as light as individual human life, unbearably light, light as a feather, as dust swirling into the air."[29] There was nothing fixed or foreordained about it. Hence it required an unremitting effort of memory. Histories of all sorts—of nations such as Czechoslovakia, of individuals such as émigrés—were forever sliding into oblivion, collapsing into forgetfulness.

The very titles of Kundera's novels pointed this second path to fidelity: *The Book of Laughter and Forgetting, The Unbearable Lightness of Being.* In the former, his heroine, "desperately trying to preserve the vanishing memories of her beloved dead husband," figured as counterpart to a people crushed by a regime of *"organized forgetting."* (With Kundera the private and the public nearly always intertwined.) In the latter, the idiocies, the ambiguities, of political posturing mirrored a process of erosion or ossification in personal attachments. But perhaps it was in *The Joke* that Kundera best evoked the slippages and the sorrow of memory. Here a return to the folk music of his native Moravia stood for fidelity to the familiar, the fragile, the precious (become so through the threat of devastation and abandonment). In an age of inability to listen, the author surmised, in an age in which "the accumulation of messages old and new" canceled "one another out," the "state of abandonment" endowed "with an irresistible *final beauty*" what had once been taken for granted.[30]

Kundera evidently enjoyed entertaining his readers with the flippant and the erotic. It was the elegiac, however, that brought out his deepest convictions, that furnished "the strongest link" binding him "to a life constantly eaten away by forgetting."[31]

Tournier was an intensely private man, Kundera a pub-
licly committed and internationally celebrated figure.
Yet under their surface dissimilarities they shared a common
attitude toward their society, their era, and their craft. They
were rebels in the sense of impatience with constraints and
labels, sophisticated in the sense of writing in a postexper-
imental mode, beyond their immediate predecessors' self-
conscious striving for novelty.

Along with sophistication went a special form of
innocence. Kundera said that his work combined in uneasy
equilibrium "remorseful nostalgia and remorseless skepticism."[32] Tournier might have written the same. The
coupling of conventionally incompatible nouns and adjec-
tives suggested the novelists' relation to the waning twentieth century. Their evocations of a vanished past betokened
innocence—yet also remorse for an inability to hold on to
what had slipped or was slipping away. Their skepticism,
remorseless in facing up to the cruel realities they saw about
them, betrayed their conviction that the past was over and
done with. They wrote with the verve of children—of children precociously and disturbingly aware of evil.

Neither subscribed to a specific ideology. Tournier might
stand more to the right, Kundera to the left; both scorned
party affiliations; both could be called liberal in the non-
doctrinaire meaning of a simple insistence on freedom. On
one point, however, this insistence went beyond a generic
loyalty to old and trusted values. On Europe's cultural unity,
on the urgency of reknitting a severed continent, they spoke
out unambiguously, explicitly, and in agreement. In Kundera's case the conviction predated the exile that deepened its
poignancy and made of it a benign obsession. With Tournier,
it derived from sudden adolescent awareness. One day in
1943 (the future novelist was nineteen), as he was joyfully
pushing toward the west the line on a wall map which
marked the advance of the Red Army, his father brought his
exultation down to earth. One might well rejoice, the older

man reminded his son, but one must weep also: Europe's "spinal column" was breaking under the shock.[33] And broken it remained.

In such a Europe, in such a world, Tournier and Kundera agreed, a novelist sensitive to the apathy and folly surrounding him was necessarily consumed by anguish—but not necessarily afraid. Both found their salvation in laughter; both scoffed at solemnity; and both, independently, hit on the same expression for conveying the kind of playfulness they had in mind: "the laughter of God," crystalline and "absolute." It was this quality of the divinely merry that they admired in the great humorists of the past, Laurence Sterne and, above all, François Rabelais.[34] The earthiness of Rabelais, the succulence of his piled-up, unflagging verbal imagery, his unabashed delight in the scatological, found an echo in their prose. It was as though Gargantuan laughter alone could encompass the absurdity of the century's last quarter.

THREE

The Torment of a Foreign Underclass

M ichel Tournier originally had intended to dedicate his volume of autobiographical reflections "to the enormous and silent mass of immigrant workers" on whom French society depended. After long hesitation he decided otherwise; those he wished to honor seemed "too numerous, too worthy of respect, too remote" from himself, and he "had no way of asking their permission to render unto them this derisory homage."[1]

With his uncanny feel for the marginal, Tournier had lighted on the most marginal people of all: the new wretched of the earth. This in itself is sufficient reason for starting a series of group analyses with them. Besides that, we may reckon the novelty of the phenomenon: in the 1960s and early 1970s, countries almost totally lacking a "melting pot" tradition found themselves obliged to absorb as best they could wave after wave of alien labor. Bewilderment ensued: perplexity on the part of the "hosts" and the still crueler perplexity of the new arrivals, sometimes euphemistically called "guests."

The magnitude of the phenomenon took people unawares. It had started quietly, almost imperceptibly, as a result of the prosperity that Western Europe had enjoyed since the mid-1950s and the consequent labor shortage. It came without much foresight or planning. Businessmen basked in euphoria, the wider public in an ostrichlike neglect of the issue and unwillingness to recognize what was occurring. Not until the onset of economic depression in late 1973 and early 1974 did governments and electorates awake from their slumbers. Then the reaction descended with brutal uniformity: country after country closed its doors to further arrivals. By that time it was too late. Something like fifteen million foreign workers (including dependents), constituting between 7 and 8 percent of the populations of France and West Germany, were already on hand. In the immediately ensuing years official encouragement of repatriation brought these totals down—but only temporarily. By the 1980s, owing to the reuniting of families and a high birth rate, a million more had been added.

The original notion on both sides had been that the workers in question, the large majority of them young men coming without families, would stay for only a few years and then, having saved enough money to set themselves up back home, return to their lands of birth. Things worked out differently. For the most part it proved impossible to save as much as expected. Individual workers grew intolerably lonely as they saw bleak year after bleak year stretching ahead. So they summoned their wives. Children soon followed. By the 1970s a process of family reunification was in full swing. "The hope of return receded into an uncertain future." Doubtless "most . . . migrants" did not "make a conscious decision to remain permanently"; the truth sank in only gradually. The realization that their move was "irreversible" came—"if at all"—when parents discovered that their offspring were speaking their adopted language more fluently than their native. "The decision to bring up children in a new country" proved the "turning point in the transition from temporary migration to settlement."[2]

Thus, what once had been a short-term foreign labor force became "a permanent ethnic minority."[3] And with this shift went the growth of its non-European (and presumably less digestible) component. Britain, France, and West Germany traversed comparable experiences. But Britain's varied from that of the Continent in that most of its non-European arrivals came without labor contracts and from Commonwealth countries where they had learned to speak English and often had acquired British citizenship. France and Germany's new ethnic minorities seemed more alien: the former's two million North Africans; the latter's million and a half Turks. These were the people who by the 1980s were riveting the attention (mostly unsympathetic) of West Europeans and who deserve particular scrutiny. (For purposes of comparison the Portuguese in France and the Italians in Germany should also figure.) The multiple trials and disappointments of those branded as socially undesirable may suggest the almost insuperable difficulty of transforming a precarious "culture of migration" into something more viable and satisfying.

A brief review may recall the interlocking handicaps under which alien workers suffered and which seared their souls. From a strictly economic standpoint, they coalesced as the lowest stratum in the societies that received them—not so much a new proletariat (their employment was too diverse for that) as an underclass distinctly marked off from the increasingly fluid and *embourgeoisé* majority. They performed the hard, dirty, dangerous, insecure jobs in the service trades, in mining, in industry, that native-born workers scorned; in simple Marxian truth, they constituted a "reserve army of labor." Nor did most of them acquire skills which could benefit their lands of origin if and when they returned. On the contrary, these lands found themselves, as in wartime, losing their most promising youth; Western Europe was enriching itself at their expense. In the starkest terms, as two early and authoritative students of the subject concluded, "labor migration" became "a form of development aid given by poor countries to rich countries."[4]

Naturally the new arrivals were miserably housed. Single males, especially in Germany, tended to find lodging in barracklike huts or hostels, constructed in haste by their employers. In France couples or families frequently built with their own hands, on nondescript, depressing urban outskirts, *bidonvilles* or shantytowns. Both types of housing were overcrowded and offered almost nothing in the way of amenities. The shantytowns, with only rudimentary plumbing or water supply, menaced the health of their inhabitants and the general public alike. But these at least provided a minimum of community life and sociability. From this standpoint it was doubtless a good thing that by the early 1980s, as families sought a more settled existence, hostels were on the decline, and shantytowns vanishing. They were replaced by virtual ghettos on the American model, concentrations in decayed quarters of inner cities from which nearly all except the elderly or marginal among the original inhabitants had departed.

It would be wrong to imply that the members of these new ethnic minorities totally lacked civic rights. Although for the most part denied citizenship and the vote, in the social and economic sphere they did not languish utterly bereft. A large proportion of them enjoyed de facto protection from summary discharge: even in times of high unemployment, as in the mid-1980s, it proved impracticable simply to fire them and to pass on their jobs to the native-born. Too many had acquired sufficient skill and adaptability to have become indispensable to the firms for which they worked; the German auto industry could not have survived without them. To cite the German example once more: in the Federal Republic, they were covered by the health, retirement, and unemployment security systems; they could organize associations, hold meetings, belong to political parties, and, above all, participate to the full in trade-union activities.[5] To be sure a number of these rights were all too often honored in the breach. More particularly those concerning associations and meetings could be—and were—drastically limited by administrative fiat, as were "freedom of movement and free choice of occupation, place of work and place of education, and protection from extradition abroad."[6] At best the situation of most foreign workers remained precarious, and individuals and families were gnawed by unremitting anxiety.

For, as their economic and social status began ever so slowly to stabilize and improve, it was in the emotional realm that they suffered most grievously. Their sense of psychic deprivation was reinforced in the early 1980s by an upsurge of popular revulsion; in Germany jokes about Turks became staple fare in schools and bars. The usual stereotyped charges made the rounds: the immigrants were dirty, noisy, uncouth. (People seldom added that for the most part they had proved themselves diligent, reliable workers.) The accusation hardest to answer was that their rate of criminality was higher than among the population at large. On this score the statistics seemed irrefutable. But a corrective was at hand. If one reckoned that young males nearly everywhere constituted the group most likely to commit crimes, and if one added that this very group was disproportionately swollen among the immigrants, then the figures came into focus. Switzerland even determined that in the case of twenty- to forty-year-old men, the native-born showed a slightly higher rate of criminality![7]

For the immigrants, however, the pervasive hostility surrounding them may have been less burdensome than tensions in their own ranks, tensions deriving from unfamiliar situations encountered within the family constellation. The vast majority of the new arrivals came from societies in which family ties were strong and the status of members was clearly defined by tradition. In France or Germany it was impossible to maintain these familiar norms. A husband whose wife also worked and whose children spoke their new language more readily than their old saw his patriarchal authority collapsing about him. A wife away all day at shop or restaurant or factory returned at night to lonely, neglected offspring, abandoned to the unreliable supervision of neighbors or older siblings. Such children, frequently shuttled back and forth between their new and their old homes, might well end up feeling like strangers in both. A social role was thrust upon them that taxed their inner resources to the limit: on the one hand, they served their parents as mediators or interpreters between two worlds; on the other, they faced a sense of deprivation even more severe than what their elders were experiencing.

The original immigrants, now reaching middle age, could cherish fond memories of their old societies and even the hope (for the most part illusory) of returning; they could also recall the desperate poverty that had virtually forced them to depart. For their children it was quite otherwise. Unable to compare an old economic situation with their new, they could not appreciate the modest advances their parents had made. On the contrary: young people entering the job market encountered greater difficulty in finding employment than had their fathers a decade or two earlier. Educationally disadvantaged, denied economic "promotion," keenly conscious of social rejection by a majority with whom they were familar at close quarters and whose language they spoke, the second generation suffered a "deeper subjective deprivation" than the first. The older generation well knew that they were and would remain Arabs or Turks. Their children were far from sure. Trapped in the shifting sands of the "culture of migration," they identified more and more with the French or Germans among whom they lived. They shared the economic and the personal aspirations of the adolescents about them. At a loss to grasp why society at large should continue to handicap them, they turned against it in bitter resentment.[8]

W/hat could be done? The alternatives seemed clear: assimilation to the culture of the native-born or maintenance of a separate, alien culture. The authorities hesitated, sometimes opting for one, sometimes for the other, sometimes for a bit of both. Germany tried the last of these, a "dual strategy" of parallel tracks whereby immigrant children received instruction in German in the regular schools and simultaneously kept up their native language in classes specially designed for their benefit. But this produced insuperable difficulties: overcrowding, a shortage of adequately trained teachers, and confused, overburdened pupils with low scholastic achievement.[9] By the early 1980s it was becoming apparent that for the short run at least the two goals were incompatible. In these circumstances, life in the new ghettos, for all its squalor, began to reveal positive features: shops, restaurants, and cafés that recalled the habits and the smells of the old country; lawyers and physicians capable of dealing with their clientele in their old language and of serving as buffers against the world outside; possibly even a mosque.[10]

A mosque: the mere word conjures up the bedrock difficulty, the religious cleavage setting apart the less assimilable of the immigrants from their hosts. Islam, now become the second religion of France, with far more adherents than Protestantism and Judaism combined, here as in Germany epitomized for the native-born the obscure, incomprehensible threat looming over them.

It was religion above all that explained why immigrants from southern Europe encountered far less hostility than Muslims from North Africa or Turkey. Both the Portuguese and the Italians were Catholics. Indeed those who came from Portugal to France—numbering a surprising 850,000 —practiced their faith so devoutly that they were warmly welcomed by the French clergy and felt no need to establish separate parishes. Closely knit, apolitical, with a reassuringly low profile, they turned their energies to maintaining an elaborate network of voluntary associations (including some 1000 soccer teams!). For them the clash of old and new allegiances was attenuated by linguistic and geographic propinquity: they found it relatively easy to learn another Latin tongue, and they acquired the habit of taking frequent trips back across the Pyrenees. At first some felt a guilty sense of betrayal on becoming French citizens. But even this vanished when, in 1981, the Portuguese parliament passed a law permitting dual nationality—an advantageous situation reinforced a half-decade later by Portugal's admission to the European Economic Community.[11]

The Italians had been the Community from the start. They might be slacker Catholics and more effervescent than the Portuguese—marginally less acceptable—but the authorities north of the mountains, in this case the German, had no way of keeping them out; citizens of a Community member state enjoyed the inestimable blessings of unrestricted movement and employment. Most of the 600,000 who took advantage of these rights came, predictably, from the impoverished back country of the Italian south.

On them we have unique documentation: the record set down by an American woman, Ann Cornelisen, who had known intimately and written three accounts of a southern Italian village and subsequently traveled to Germany to look up old acquaintances gone north. Her verdict was unequivocal: the change had been for the better. In Germany the new arrivals had learned that a government could issue regulations worth obeying, since they were enforced with "a modicum of honesty and equality." For the first time they had entered into true friendships, uncontaminated by spurious family loyalty and mutual suspicion. In brief, most of them were glad they had come. "Emigration," the author concluded, "with all its brutalities and its discriminations and its wrenches," had given them "the only chance they ever had or ever" would "have for a decent life."[12]

Of how many North Africans or Turks could anyone have written that? France and Germany's prime "undesirables" had in common their exotic manners, their Muslim faith, and their contribution (mostly unappreciated) to their host countries' demographic balance. (Without them, to put matters approximately, the French population would have remained stationary, the German decreased.) Yet for all their similarities, the problem in France and that in Germany diverged on a number of key points, with the French marginally closer to solution. Perhaps most important, Arabs and Berbers from North Africa appeared and felt themselves less alien in the Parisian industrial suburbs than did Turks in the Ruhr. After all, they had moved to the capital of the imperial power that had once ruled over them. As early as the interwar period many of their like had already crossed the Mediterranean, and they themselves had frequently learned French in their old homes. (Few Turks spoke German before their arrival.) A colonial past apparently was better than no shared past. Moreover, as many as half a million partially assimilated Muslims needed to be added to the North African total, if one were to count veterans and their families who had received asylum after fighting on the French side in the Algerian war of independence. The migrants came from three different countries—Algeria, Morocco, Tunisia—with differing colonial and postliberation histories. And the variations in their personal fortunes allowed Frenchmen of good will to detect crevices in an ostensibly monolithic dilemma through which hope might peep through.

Of these both the most eminent and the most eloquent was Bernard Stasi. A former minister of centrist persuasion, he ascribed his lack of ethnic prejudice to his own mixed origins, Catalan-Italian on his father's side, Cuban on his mother's. For him the emotion-laden expression *métissage* (loosely translatable as miscegenation) held no terrors. On the contrary, he found the coexistence of diverse populations perfectly natural. Bolder still, he viewed it as an ancient and admirable aspect of his country's tradition and a source of rejuvenation for the future.

Conscious of the upper-bourgeois privilege he enjoyed of living comfortably buffered against the new arrivals, Stasi readily admitted that he had no right to preach moral lessons to those who dwelt in crowded quarters and were "exasperated by the noise emanating . . . from the twelve members of the Moroccan family . . . in the apartment next door" (or by "the window panes shattered, the tires punctured" at the hands of juvenile delinquents). He simply pleaded with his countrymen to recognize that no easy solution could be found and that those Moroccans could not be kicked out and sent "home." So, he reminded his readers, had it always been. By far the least densely populated of the great nations of Western Europe, decade after decade France had provided room and a minimum welcome for wave on wave of immigrants. If one went back three generations, more than a third its population, like Stasi himself, proved to be of such an origin. Among the major industrial countries of the West, the United States and Canada alone harbored a higher immigrant percentage.[13]

By and large, Stasi argued, French society had successfully "integrated" its new arrivals. (He preferred this word to "assimilated," which seemed to convey a complete abandonment of old cultural allegiances.) To do the same for the North Africans, he knew, presented a graver challenge than France had yet faced. But it also offered an opportunity: an opportunity to reaffirm its tradition of hospitality while setting an example for the rest of Europe. On the one hand, these Muslims needed permission from on high to "root themselves" within their old culture in their new soil; the state might even agree to build for them mosques and schools where the Koran would be taught. On the other, that same state should extend to them the full rights of French citizenship. At one and the same time the authorities should pursue the apparently incompatible goals of preserving "national social cohesion" and respecting the right of the new arrivals "to be different." If France could manage this, Stasi concluded, his country would be opening itself out to a new, unsuspected world, a world whose future lay in a progressive process of "cultural *métissage*."[14]

While a great many North Africans might well have greeted Stasi's book with joy and relief, only a small, though possibly growing, minority of his countrymen went so far as he. Yet in this respect, the French were unquestionably more broad-minded than the Germans. (France produced a frankly xenophobic and covertly racist National Front, which in the parliamentary elections of 1986 polled nearly 10 percent of the vote; in the Federal Republic such attitudes were entrenched in the ruling Christian Democratic Union itself.) Few among the Germans did more than admit that the Federal Republic had become, as France had always been, "a land of immigration." And most of these continued to think of the Turks as irretrievably alien, with a "mentality oscillating somewhere between stone age and welfare state," a mentality exacerbated by activist religious leaders. Even well-inclined Germans noted with trepidation that Turks accounted for 30 percent of all foreign workers (at least twice the Italian percentage) and their offspring for *half* the foreign children born in the Federal Republic.[15]

These were the original reactions of the "hosts." By the mid-1980s evidence of both heightened awareness and growing sympathy began to appear. The most sensational sign of change came in the form of a best-selling book, *Ganz Unten* (Right at the Bottom). The work of a well-known reporter who had dyed his moustache black, put on shabby clothes, and for two years passed himself off as a Turk called Ali, it had already sold two million copies within four months of its publication in late 1985 and was ranking as the biggest success of postwar literary history. Readers of all ages and political persuasions eagerly devoured the account of the exploitation and insult, the humiliation and danger, to which "Ali" had been subjected.

The author, Günter Wallraff, took as his theme the hatred or at best indifference he had encountered among the Germans. But the very success of his book seemed to belie, at least in part, its central thesis. Employers, trade-union leaders, and government officials rushed to defend themselves against its charges. Representatives of the Left, both old and new, ever on the alert for residues of fascism and racism, found in the book grist for their own mill. Even authentic German working people, supposedly without exception contemptuous of the Turks, began to identify with Ali's tribulations, since they too could imagine themselves falling to the bottom in a time of economic uncertainty and high unemployment.

Wallraff's protagonists, the Turks, tended to split along generational lines. The older bought copies, had their German-speaking children translate excerpts for them, and took satisfaction in being at last described as something higher than *Untermenschen*. The younger read into Ali's plight, as Wallraff militantly depicted it, a call for self-reliance, organization, and mutual defense, the better to resist the pressure of the majority.[16] Both generations evinced gratitude that a German had done his best, had undergone far worse than his fellow citizens could have stomached, to present a bitter confrontation of cultures from the Turkish standpoint.

Yet even his was not quite an insider's view. This the inquiring German could find in a series of short stories and vignettes by a major Turkish writer, Fakir Baykurt, published in translation the previous year under the title *Nachtschicht* (Night-Shift). Baykurt's tales ranged from Anatolia to Germany and back, as so many Turks and the author himself had done. The son of a poor peasant, he had battled his way to literacy and higher education, including even a stint in the

45

United States. In his own country he had more than once suffered imprisonment for his attacks on authoritarianism in high places. Expelled from his job as a teacher, he had turned to writing to support his family, soon becoming a celebrated figure and a source of inspiration to his countrymen. As early as the 1960s he had begun to concern himself with emigration and its effect on Turkish society. By 1979 he too had become an emigrant. The 1980s found him in the Ruhr industrial city of Duisburg, serving his people as an officially sponsored educational adviser.[17]

Baykurt's thirteen collected stories began, appropriately, "home" in Anatolia. The first portrayed a wife driven to despair by the approaching end of her husband's leave from his job in Germany; having burned his return air ticket, she threatened him with becoming "a whore" if he left. Another told of a miner, deep in a shaft, suddenly bursting into wild, exultant, heartbreakingly nostalgic song; when asked by the bewildered supervising engineer why he was "screaming" so, a comrade replied that he was suffering from toothache. In a third story a different miner, this one mortally injured, took comfort in the quiet, unobtrusive sympathy of a Turkish doctor and in the injunction that his body not be flown to Anatolia, as had become the practice, but should be interred among the flowers of a German cemetery, where he and his like now belonged. In a fourth a summons to the telephone, which turned out to be nothing more than an appeal for a contribution to village embellishment back home, reduced its recipient, convinced that the unprecedented event spelled expulsion, to an icy sweat of helpless dread. In a fifth a Turkish woman, valiantly combating inner urgency and the unavailability of the appropriate facilities in a crowded official waiting room, was finally obliged to resort to the men's toilet—to the profound distress of her fellow Turks and mutters of "indecent" and "insolence" from the Germans standing about.[18]

Now and then, however, Baykurt introduced into his

stories a humane German who enjoyed good relations with the Turks he knew. One such was depicted as good-humoredly shrugging off a tragicomic error his favorite subordinate had made on returning from a trip to Anatolia. The Turk in question had brought back as gifts two tapestries, the first, a forest scene with a deer, for his German boss, the second, a view of minarets and a mosque, for the profoundly religious father of his prospective daughter-in-law. Unaccountably he had mixed up the packages. After hours of panic, a consoling thought came to him: he could explain to his benevolent supervisor how it was possible "to lose one's wits" in so strange a land and enlist his help in setting matters right.[19] The imbroglio epitomized Baykurt as a storyteller: lightly ironical, sympathetic without sentimentality or anger, exploiting an apparently trivial incident as a microcosm of the larger issues vexing Turk and German alike.

From his work, for all its understatement, the attentive reader could piece together the ethos of a superhuman effort to preserve a minimum of personal dignity in disorienting and humiliating circumstances. Baykurt's Turks prided themselves on the "purity" their ritual ablutions betokened; they found Europeans morally slack, immodest, shameless. For them the capacity to feel ashamed ranked as a cardinal virtue, as did patience and endurance. Stoical in degradation, they still believed that as good, reliable workers they deserved better treatment. Whatever security they enjoyed, they recognized, hung by a slender thread. But they had their tightly knit families to sustain them and, beyond that, as Baykurt noted again and again, the assurance that their destiny lay in Allah's hands. And if disaster struck, they knew that their friends would spring to their aid in a phalanx of mutual solidarity. No unprejudiced Westerner, after reading and pondering Baykurt's book, could afford any longer to ease his conscience with the ancient, outworn stereotype of "the unspeakable Turk."

Neither type of Muslim, whether North African or Turk, gave much evidence of revolutionary stirrings. Too many feared expulsion as "illegals." The overriding goal of the immigrant worker, Muslim and European alike, was far more modest and down-to-earth: simple recognition as a human being. In that sense he too could be called "sophisticated." This, at least, was true of the older generation. The younger was a different matter. As the 1980s drew to a close, it was still too early to tell where the anger of youth would eventually find an outlet. Most French and Germans feared it; the latter took to calling it a "social time bomb."[20]

Yet native-born young people showed signs of reaching out in sympathy to the children of the immigration. In France they organized a movement called SOS Racisme, whose very name explained its aim, and which in the summer of 1985 drew 300,000 to a rally in the Place de la Concorde. For adolescents of this persuasion there seemed no alternative to the program that Bernard Stasi had advanced the year before: full integration; full civil rights, including the vote; and the infinitely precious right "to be different."

A Turkish professor teaching in Germany—a rare specimen, as one may well imagine—expressed the problem succinctly. Addressing a meeting in Hamburg called to protest the murder of a young Turk, he called for a moratorium on hatred. He and his countrymen, he explained, now acknowledged Germany as the land in which they had settled and the society to which they wished to belong. In return they pleaded for acceptance and "equality in all spheres." Only if that were granted, would it be "possible . . . to reap friendship instead of enmity." Only then would it be possible for "Germans and national minorities—despite their different cultures and religions—to live together in the Federal Republic in the solidarity of good neighbors."[21]

FOUR

The Reassertion of Historic Cultures: The Case of Wales

"At last, the Breton problem exists!" a local autonomist leader is supposed to have exclaimed on hearing in August 1945 the news of Hiroshima. A quarter-century later a fellow-Breton undertook to elucidate the cryptic utterance. Just as the dropping of the atomic bomb had demonstrated the obsolescence of the European nation-state—and hence the possibility of finally lending a sympathetic ear to the grievances of Bretons and their like—so the student insurrection of May 1968 had revealed that Europe's youth could "no longer be stopped in its tracks" by a patriotic, martial appeal to discipline.[1] With the liberation of Algeria six years earlier, even the era of colonial wars (except for Americans) had ended. The centralized nation-state of the past had founded its raison d'être on a military imperative. That imperative had ceased to function.

Such was one of a number of reasons why in the 1970s regional demands for self-government suddenly (and often unexpectedly) came to the fore. Among them were growing discontent with rigid, anonymous bureaucratic rule, the inhumanity of urban living, and a corresponding yearning for rural values. In a longer perspective one could argue that ethnic cleavages which once had been overshadowed by class antagonisms began to emerge after a quarter-century of welfare-state reforms had mitigated or blurred those antagonisms. One might even go so far as to assert that ethnic movements might "be replacing organizations based on class, and not, as before, simply inserting themselves into the interstices of a political system whose structures" remained "fixed by the old categories."[2]

In common with foreign workers, the leaders of such movements viewed themselves as marginal folk. But the resemblance went no further: their marginal or minority status differed radically from that of Turks or Arabs. Far from being new arrivals, they were old, old residents—older than the majority of the nation in which they dwelt, remnants, in the most celebrated cases, of peoples which had once constituted that majority. Nor did they languish at the bottom of the social pyramid. They might (and frequently did) complain of economic neglect and cultural discrimination on the part of the central government; they might strive to draw mass support from the peasantry and the working class. But they themselves usually sprang from the solid middle class or from professional families. In their stubborn pride in their own "difference," they formed an eccentric variety of elite. Language figured as the most prominent feature of this difference. But not necessarily: in one or two cases, notably that of Scotland, language scarcely mattered; in others, many of the local leaders, unable to speak a "dying" tongue, were obliged to limit their linguistic loyalty to nostalgia for it and to encouraging the younger generation to learn it. In Western Europe, as in the United States, a new consciousness of ethnicity found children turning to their grandparents for scraps of folk memories and a half-forgotten speech.

This chapter will focus on France and Britain. Why these two nations and not others? At first glance Spain would seem to be a more obvious choice. After all, the grievances of Basques and Catalans stood out more distinctly and as more solidly based than anything in Britain or France. But for that very reason they were easier to redress. For post-Franco Spanish democracy, the simple imperative was to restore to

Catalonia and the Basque provinces the right of self-government granted by the Republic four decades earlier. The fact that a militant and violent minority in the latter rejected the resulting settlement might provoke grief and vexation; it did not alter the view both of most Basques and of the dominant Castilians that King Juan Carlos and his advisers had done the right thing.

Italy and the German Federal Republic ranked linguistically and in respect to local ethnic consciousness as more homogeneous than either France or Britain. Postwar Italy early on had done its best to satisfy its disaffected provinces—border areas of German or French speech, the islands of Sicily and Sardinia—with autonomy statutes tailored to the individual case. Germany suffered from no such worries. Within its shrunken boundaries it harbored virtually no native-born minorities. Moreover, its federal structure facilitated the untroubled expression of whatever particularist sentiment might from time to time bubble up—witness the vast popularity and long-term rule over Bavaria of that stocky, ebullient, irrepressible *echt bayrisch* leader in *Lederhosen,* Franz-Josef Strauss!

So we are left with the two nations that had the longest and most firmly rooted traditions of democracy. This apparent paradox can be readily explained by their centralism. In neither Spain nor Italy nor Germany did a single metropolis so dominate economic and cultural life as did Paris and London. In the 1970s France and Britain alike faced a tangle of local ethnic problems that good will alone seemed unable to resolve. Their efforts to do so for the most part came to naught. Yet, once again paradoxically, in the following decade those very problems began to lose their urgency.

" The Republic one and indivisible": so generations of nineteenth- and twentieth-century Frenchmen had been trained to think of their country; so had they expressed their resolve to impose unity and cultural conformity on the heterogeneous territories, figuring on the map as a tidy "hexagon," which a long succession of monarchs had acquired in the course of pushing toward what came to be regarded as France's natural frontiers: the Atlantic and the Mediterranean, the Pyrenees, the Alps, and the Rhine. The last of these the French never succeeded in stabilizing as a boundary; but here, as elsewhere, they had advanced with little respect for local language and loyalty. It was left to subsequent cohorts of schoolmasters to follow on the military in a vast mopping-up operation. Ruthless with a good conscience, convinced that they were carrying out, in the "Metropole" as overseas, a noble "civilizing mission," devoted, underpaid teachers drove the mother tongue out of their pupils' minds, not by physical violence but by the equally effective devices of shame and humiliation.

Once again in the wake of the events of May, the general-president, Charles de Gaulle, at long last became aware of this festering legacy. In early 1969 he proposed a devolution of power to regional authorities, a proposal that ended both his presidency and an era in French history. He had promised to resign if the measure failed to carry in a popular referendum. It did fail, and he kept his promise. Most local ethnic leaders had manifested little enthusiasm for the proposal. They found it both too timid and, in the regional boundaries it drew, too little in accord with their own aspirations. The same was true of a second such effort, which went into effect piecemeal over the next dozen years.

In 1977 *Le Monde* published a "linguistic map of France." The fact that a highly respected newspaper should have done so at all was a sign of changed times. Equally surprising was the revelation the map offered even to Frenchmen who considered themselves well educated. What struck their startled gaze was that little more than half the country could be reckoned French in tradition and in its original speech. The rest consisted of no less than seven subcultures.

Five of these, all borderlands, amounted to splinters or spillovers from adjacent countries. Two small areas at the extreme northern and extreme southern tips of France scarcely figured in the debate on particularism: to the north a remnant of Flemings, soon to become the majority in Belgium, had virtually lost their language by the turn of the century; the same had happened to France's Catalans a half-century later. At the other end of the Pyrenees, however, the Basques were quite a different matter. Less effervescent than the far more numerous Basques in Spain, they nonetheless clung tenaciously to a speech whose affiliations still lay veiled in mystery, a speech progressively pushed inland and toward the countryside, as hordes of tourists and vacationers overwhelmed the coastal cities of the southwest.

All three peoples—Flemings, Catalans, and Basques—complained at the very least of insensitivity and neglect in faraway Paris. Much less did the Alsatians. Closely linked to the capital, economically sound, and with members of its elite securely ensconced in France's social and administrative establishment, Alsace benefited from the sympathy inspired by its troubled history of having passed twice under German rule in a seventy-five-year period. Few doubted that its underlying loyalty had remained French throughout, although a large proportion of its inhabitants still spoke a dialect of German. It was symptomatic of the preferential treatment Alsace received from Paris that here alone, long before the matter of cultural grievances had come to public awareness, did the authorities tacitly decide to wink at violations of the press law forbidding publication in foreign languages.

Fifth and finally was Corsica, an island undeniably Italian in physical aspect and speech. Although the least Gallicized of France's minority peoples, hardly any Corsicans proposed union with Italy. Such a transfer of allegiance would have meant renouncing the benefits they received from membership in the French community—public works and public jobs, more particularly in the police force—in effect, sinking to the socioeconomic level of the neighboring island of Sardinia. The Corsicans wanted what Spain had granted its minority peoples in the period 1977–78: a devolution of authority greater than that offered in the current French provisions for regionalization. Fortunately, as in Spain, a solution lay ready to hand. Alone among the newly defined regions, Corsica's boundaries coincided with what the local autonomists had demanded. After successive French ministries had been shaken out of their lethargy by a wave of terrorist attacks, the Socialist government of François Mitterrand in 1982 instituted a mini-parliament, or regional assembly, for the island, following it up with the establishment of a Corsican university. The assembly got off to a shaky and faction-ridden start. Far less than the sovereign parliament to which a separatist minority of Corsicans aspired, at least it was functioning.

So much for borderlands. It remains to consider two territories, utterly diverse in nature, whose cultural spheres lay entirely within France's frontiers and which attracted the greatest amount of attention from the French themselves.

The first, Occitanie, a name dating from the Middle Ages and adopted again in the 1970s by the press and the public, embraced most of the country's southern third. Its language, Occitan, the language which used "oc" rather than "oui" for "yes," over the course of seven centuries had splintered into a congeries of local dialects. It was unclear how many still spoke them; certainly very few used them as the normal vehicle of expression. But a sentimental attachment remained. Occitan, gentler and more succulent than French and closely related to Catalan, hung on as a rallying point for southern "difference."

It had not always been thus. In the twelfth century, when the south had ranked as more civilized than the north, Occitan, known to history as Provençal, had won literary distinction as the language of the Troubadours. In the century following, the Albigensian Crusade had struck this civilization a mortal blow, scattering it or driving it underground. But it was not true, as once was thought, that the "crusaders" from the north had imposed the French language in a matter of decades. Nor had the French kings tried to do so. At the close of the Middle Ages, Occitan still functioned as the normal language both of speech and of writing throughout most of the south. Not until a royal edict of 1539 made French obligatory for all public transactions and legal documents, did a slow crumbling of the old tongue become an avalanche. Yet as late as the mid-eighteenth century, a highly literate southerner confessed that he and his like continued to think in Occitan before they spoke or wrote in French.[3]

Threatened with reduction to a peasant idiom, the old language was rescued a century later through the efforts of the poet Frédéric Mistral and his associates. They wrote in the literary tongue called Provençal and correspondingly limited their range to the southeast (or Provence) and to the educated public. It was left to young enthusiasts of the 1970s to attempt a popularly based revival extending to the whole of Occitanie. This too, however, failed to reach very far beyond the ranks of the culturally aspiring. Its most tangible achievements were the creation of centers for Occitan studies at the universities of Toulouse and Montpellier and a well-attended set of summer courses at Nîmes. The Occitan movement never developed a true political base: the area in question was too vast and too diverse to constitute a true "nation." It remained a diffused, amorphous cultural protest against the domination of a third of the country by the rest—not unlike that of the Scots, with the roles of north and south reversed.

The Breton peninsula, locale of the second subculture wholly within France, had lost its independence at the end of the fifteenth century, not through conquest but through the marriage of its heiress to two successive French kings. Breton patriots recalled with anger this historic peculiarity, since less than half a century later their ancestors had been tricked into accepting the conversion of a merely personal union into incorporation with France—an act, significantly enough, coming just seven years before the edict imposing French as the administrative language of the entire country. Yet those same local patriots were obliged to recognize that Brittany had prospered under French rule; down to the late eighteenth century its seaports had ranked as world centers of commerce.

The next century and a half produced more authentic grievances: unrelenting pressure on the Breton language, economic decay, and demographic stagnation. (Apologists for Brittany liked to point out that a province whose population had once equaled the Dutch had become, by the mid-twentieth century, only a fifth as many.)[4] Two World Wars brought a further (and possibly final) increment of pain. In the First, Breton troops suffered disproportionately high losses at the front—not, it should be added, through any deliberate policy of treating them as "mere cannon fodder," but simply by virtue of the fact that conscripts from a peasant society such as Brittany's went straight to the infantry and to the trenches. In the Second, a minority of Bretons paid dearly for their tragic error of looking to the German occupiers for redress of their grievances. A few had behaved as true collaborators, but more—and this was the memory that rankled—had perished in the postwar purge as "Breton patriots pure and simple."[5]

From decade to decade and into the 1980s these grievances spawned a bewildering welter of autonomist (and less often) separatist movements and parties, none of which, even in the favorable political climate of the 1970s, rallied mass support or made much of a showing at the polls. Why such splintering? Why did the self-constituted spokesmen for Brittany lack the clear aims to which a large following might have responded? The chief answer would seem to be the region's split linguistic personality. Eastern Brittany, Haute Bretagne, had never been Breton in speech. But it was here that the old and the new capitals, the two universities, and the rudiments of a modern economy were located. It was only to the west, in Basse Bretagne, that people spoke Breton—a Celtic tongue closely related to Welsh and, more remotely, to the Gaelic of Ireland and far western Scotland. But how many spoke it? In the absence of a linguistic census, the government's estimates and those of local militants diverged wildly. Surely the much-cited figure of half a million, one-fifth the total population, was far too high.

Stubbornly, against hopeless odds, the same militants strove to preserve Breton speech and even to implant it in Haute Bretagne. In 1977 they received assistance from on high when President Giscard d'Estaing proclaimed a "cultural charter" that at long last took the lid off the study of Breton language and civilization in the French educational system. Eight years later his successor, François Mitterrand, began the same process for the country's other ethnic subcultures. But these concessions may have come too late. By that time the autonomist wave was already ebbing, the wider public was losing interest. There remained the shrinking minority of true militants—steadfast and unappeasable.

Compared with Brittany, Wales, its sister land to the north, looked like a success story. Although slightly smaller and scarcely more populous—2.8 as against 2.5 million—its inhabitants enjoyed a degree of cultural unity that the Bretons lacked. They also ranked as Britain's leading native ethnic minority, a status the Bretons never attained within the French state.

The distinction had not always been so marked. In medieval times the two lands, linked by speech across the intervening peninsula of Cornwall, had shared the misty legacy of Arthurian legend. By the Hundred Years' War, however, their histories had begun to diverge. Brittany's became entwined with that of France; Wales made a final stand for independence under Owain Glyndŵr (Shakespeare's magician prince, Owen Glendower). And when, three-quarters of a century later, in 1485, a Welshman, Henry Tudor, acceded to the English throne, his countrymen rejoiced at their good fortune. Their euphoria proved short-lived. Five decades later, in 1536, Henry VIII, Henry Tudor's son, annexed Wales to England, much as the French king had just done with Brittany.

Still a difference between the two lands remained, a difference epitomized by passionate devotion to a language which, in contrast to Breton, was spoken throughout Wales. As far back as the twelfth century we hear of an old man rebuking a king on the march—Henry II, who had inquired whether Welsh resistance to English overlordship would long endure. It could "never be totally subdued," the old man had replied, "unless the wrath of God" had concurred; and no "other language," he added, should answer on Judgment Day "for this corner of the earth." Thus the Welsh held onto what has been described as "the oldest living literary language in Europe." Thus, "among all the minority peoples . . . swallowed willy-nilly into the authority of the great Nation-States, none . . . remained more distinctly themselves."[6] For four centuries, during which the history of Wales seemed to go underground, its inhabitants, with a maddening blend of the staunch and the devious, thwarted the efforts of their more simpleminded masters to Anglicize them.

In this resistance they received aid from an unexpected source, from the daughter of the king who had snuffed out their independence. A generation before the English had *their* King James version, Queen Elizabeth I ordered the translation of the Bible into Welsh. Unwittingly she extended to her recalcitrant subjects a slim thread of linguistic and cultural continuity. From then on, the Bible functioned as the unquestioned criterion of standard Welsh prose. It also encouraged a home-bred religiosity which in the eighteenth century flared into the mass movement of the Methodist awakening.

By the middle of the century following, three-quarters of the Welsh had deserted Anglican "church" for evangelical "chapel," and the latter had become both the dominant force in Welsh society and a further mark of distinction from the English. In the meantime another new (and this time totally indigenous) institution had materialized: the literary and musical assembly called Eisteddfod. To this day people smile at its bogus-antique druids and bards, its unique combination of fervor and carnival, but it is difficult to deny the authentic Welshness of a gathering that celebrated the two national passions, poetry and song.

One could go on listing the nineteenth- and early twentieth-century manifestations of revived ethnic pride —not forgetting the foundation of the regional colleges which in 1893 coalesced into the University of Wales. The point that must be stressed is that cultural preceded political awakening; and so the emphasis has remained. Not until the suffrage extension of 1884 gave the vote to the bulk of Welshmen—the *werin,* as they were affectionately called— did modern Welsh politics begin. And then it took the distinctive form of mass allegiance to a single party, first to the Liberals, then to Labour. During the Liberal dominance, the power of the Anglicized squirearchy withered and died; with the advent of Labour, "chapel" too more gradually lost its hold on the country. These shifts mirrored rapid changes in Welsh life: movement from north to south and from farm to mine or city, with the Liberals riding a pre-1914 wave of prosperity in Cardiff and the coalfields nearby, and Labour drawing votes during the interwar years from those buffeted by economic collapse and massive unemployment.[7]

Yet to ardent Welshmen even Labour seemed too far away and too centralist in its ideology to give full heed to their country's sufferings. Such as these in 1925 founded a nationalist party, Plaid Cymru. Its leaders naturally spoke of the misery they saw about them, but they put their primary stress on the preservation of Welsh culture and language, which were steadily losing ground in the very areas where the population was now concentrated. For nearly half a century Plaid Cymru languished as little more than a party of middle-class intellectuals with a following restricted to the rugged and still Welsh-speaking northwest. Not until the late 1960s did it become a serious political force, reaching its high-water mark in the election of October 1974, when it won three of Wales's thirty-six seats in the House of Commons.

It was one thing to score a handful of victories in the Welsh backcountry, another to win over the bulk of the people to the nationalist cause. Virtually no one wanted secession from the United Kingdom; the majority were at best tepid about home rule. What a great many wanted was to preserve a distinctively Welsh way of life. But was political activity the path to so doing? Most people evidently thought not. For most Welshmen the primary concern was to see to it that their language did not die out: *their* language in the sense that, though they might no longer speak it, they still cherished it as *the* symbol of Welshness, endowed with something approaching holiness. "We have no doubt," said an official report of 1981 in urging adequate funds for broadcasting in the language, "that it is the will and wish of the overwhelming majority of the people of Wales that the Welsh language should survive as a living tongue." But it took a threat of fasting to death on the part of a "saintly" nationalist leader to wrest from the British government a television channel exclusively Welsh in speech![8]

By the census of 1981 such single-minded insistence was beginning to tell. Earlier censuses had shown a steady decline in the number of Welsh speakers—from 28 percent in 1951 to 20 percent two decades later. By 1981 (19 percent) this slippage had notably slowed. And, what was more to the point, for the first time in history the percentage of Welsh-speaking children had risen. For this achievement the foundation and popularity of schools that taught fluency in Welsh deserved the credit; even in the Anglicized south, parents preferred them for their strict discipline and committed teaching staff.

Yet at best the progress was a holding operation. The traditional foundations that had once buttressed the language—village life and chapel—were inexorably eroding. The notion of Wales itself, its leading modern historian wryly noted, threatened to lapse "into a mere metaphysical construct adopted for intellectual recreation . . . A contemporary, living Wales," he added, could not "survive on myths alone." The Welsh needed "to reconstruct a usable past as the springboard for a bearable future."[9]

Where was one to turn? The writer did not specify. He, although bilingual, wrote in English. So did a lively cohort of novelists, poets, and essayists. To show oneself a loyal Welshman, it seemed, did not require mastery of the ancestral language; after all, the equally notable band who stuck to the old tongue were condemning themselves thereby to an audience of a few hundred thousand, when by shifting to English they might have reached out to millions in Britain and overseas. And the majority, lacking a command of Welsh, had no choice. Such had been true of the poet Dylan Thomas, who for many, if not most, of his countless readers, ranked as the epitome of the Welshman.

Anglo-Welsh writers figured as a resource still largely untapped. Until quite recently, those who adhered to the Welsh language alone inclined to view them with suspicion or even hostility. But in fact the two types resembled each other more closely than either seemed to realize. For the most part they shared a common background. Together they sprang from families of "schoolmasters, colliers, ministers of religion, shopkeepers." Together they recalled the heritage of "religious nonconformity and political radicalism" that had contributed so markedly to making Wales a land of "social homogeneity," a land with a "lack of class consciousness."

Some Anglo-Welsh writers were "Anglo only by the skin of their teeth"—in the sense that they belonged to "the first generation of their families . . . unable to speak Welsh themselves." To be sure, although still political radicals, most had rejected the dominant religion of a country where chapels had long served as "custodians of the language and of a distinctive way of life." Yet they wrote of Welsh themes and saw themselves "first as Welshmen." Or that at least was how their most discerning and sympathetic defender thought they should behave. "The only English thing about an Anglo-Welsh writer," he concluded, "ought to be his language."[10]

"Out of the gloom comes Merlin urging a more tolerant assessment . . . of the need to keep the non-Welsh-speaking Celts within the . . . fold." Thus half-mockingly wrote Gwyn Thomas, perhaps the most talented storyteller among the Anglo-Welsh. Paradigmatic of his breed, he came of a transitional coal-mining family in which the older children spoke Welsh and he, the youngest, English. Throughout his life he wrote with hardheaded compassion for the people among whom he had grown up. By the time he reached his fifties, the mines too, no longer able to make a profit, were shutting down, gone the way of village and chapel. But Thomas refused to succumb to an all too familiar nostalgia: "The banners have been furled and put away. A quieter, healing hedonism has set off a proliferation of bingo and drinking clubs as impressive in its way as the almost solid wall of conventicles and trade union lodges brought into being by the psychoses of poverty and dread. And just as well."[11]

A gentler Wales? In 1982 it was "declared the first nuclear-free country in Europe, all its county councils having agreed never to allow nuclear weapons on their soil."[12] A Wales with its old ways eroded, yet with its Welshness perpetuated by people unable to speak its language, a Wales performing a new role as model for the Western world?

In view of the foregoing it should be apparent that the Scots—nearly twice as numerous as the Welsh—did not truly belong in the category of deprived ethnic minorities. Yet the two tended to be lumped together in English minds: their nationalist movements rose and fell in the same period, with the Scottish variety apparently posing the greater threat to Britain's political cohesion.

Since the Act of Union of 1707 Scotland had retained a clear identity and a set of institutions distinctive from England's that Wales totally lacked.[13] Although it had lost its parliament, it had kept its established church (the Presbyterian Kirk) and its own legal and educational systems. It had ancient universities, plus secondary schools that taught a higher percent of the population (and at a higher level) than was the case south of the border. It had in Edinburgh a cultural capital that could hold its own against London, more particularly during the late eighteenth-century Enlightenment and the flowering of Romanticism in the century following. And the world-renowned writers Scotland produced—a David Hume, an Adam Smith, a Sir Walter Scott—suffered from no doubts as to their linguistic allegiance. However lilting their speech and however tinged with "Scotticisms," it was unquestionably English, and in its literary form indistinguishable from the London-Oxford-Cambridge standard.[14] Only in the Western Highlands and the Isles did Scots continue to speak Gaelic, a minority that by the 1980s had fallen to a tiny 1½ percent.

In the absence of linguistic and cultural grievances, from what, one may wonder, was Scotland suffering? Chiefly from its relative poverty and its sense of economic neglect by the bureaucrats in far-off London. A Scottish Nationalist Party, launched by severe depression in and around Glasgow in the 1930s, voiced the same kind of complaints that figured in Wales as burning, if secondary, issues. Four decades later the party found its chance: the discovery of exploitable North

Sea oil—"our" oil, the Nationalists began to call it. This windfall right off their shores seemed to lift the realistic constraints against a vote for "going it alone."[15] After all, such people reasoned, if a neighboring country with access to the oil, Norway, whose inhabitants numbered four million to Scotland's five, was about to become the richest nation per capita in the Western world, why couldn't their country do the same? In the election of October 1974—the same election that marked the apogee of Welsh protest—the Scottish Nationalist made a great leap forward, displacing the Tories as Scotland's second party.

At this point the governing Labourites in London took alarm. Dependent for their majority on a massive lead in what they called their "Celtic fringe," they cast about for ways to appease the disgruntled Scots and Welsh. The plan they concocted illogically linked a pair of heterogeneous political and ideological constellations. They proposed for Wales and Scotland alike a devolution of extensive powers (more extensive in the second case) to an assembly, or miniparliament, much like the one Catalonia had just received and Corsica was shortly to be granted. There followed what few had foreseen. In referenda held in early March 1979 both measures failed to carry. Both Welsh and Scots (if one reckons in an abstention rate of more than a third of the electorate) gave unmistakable evidence of reluctance "to embrace anything that remotely resembled any form of separatism." Labour's national leadership had succumbed to a "massive miscalculation."[16] In the general election that ensued, the party responsible for the devolution proposal was soundly beaten. The Welsh and Scottish nationalists shared in the defeat: the former lost one of the three seats they had gained five years earlier; the latter all but two of what had once been eleven. Nearly a decade later, in the election of 1987 these parties improved their position only marginally.

The debacle of devolution in Britain may suggest a wider lesson. By the 1980s, in Britain as in France, public attention was turning elsewhere—for example, to the problem of foreign workers. Home rule was less on people's lips than it had been in the previous decade. There was less talk of reconstituting the European Economic Community's parliament in such a way as to give representation to old ethnic groups, notably the Basques, split in two by a national frontier.[17]

To some extent we may ascribe this loss of interest to a piecemeal redress of specific and recognized grievances; the establishment of a television channel in a local language is a case in point. But this very example brings to mind the inevitable backlash: the indignation of people, frequently the majority, at the "waste" of such a channel on a "dying speech" of the aged. Paradoxically, a good many of the protesters were old themselves. The misfortune of beautiful lands such as the Basque country and Brittany and Wales was that they lured not just tourists, who spent only part of the year, but also the retired, seeking a permanent home in scenic and tranquil surroundings. Long-settled inhabitants might welcome such new arrivals as a blessing, as the classic remedy for underdeveloped regions—in short, for the money they brought in. They brought with it, however, "an alien element into communities struggling to keep their own life going."[18]

Devolution evidently was not the answer. It might work in Catalonia and in homogeneous, sea-girt Corsica. Elsewhere populations had become too diverse; too many simply did not care about the historic culture of the land where they had settled. And their number was growing. The best local militants could do—and this was no trifling assignment—was to keep aloft the notion of a pluralism of loyalties, the notion that one could feel oneself Welsh, British, *and* European without inner conflict. After all, this was what the ecologically minded Greens in Germany were preaching. It was what novelists such as Tournier and Kundera were proposing, when they longed for a reunited continent, with room for infinite diversity inside. The obverse of a more closely knit Europe was a Europe in which the nation-state loomed less large, with the new loyalty above it and the old loyalty below it deemed equally worthy of respect and affection.

FIVE

The Pope and His Antagonists

"How many divisions does the Pope have?" Stalin's military-minded query at the height of the Second World War seemed unanswerable in the heat of battle. But four decades and four popes later, Western Europeans began to realize that the Holy Father might in fact have quite a number. After all, the Catholic Church had long ranked as the object of loyalty most visibly challenging the exclusive claims of the nation-state. And the man who mounted the papal throne in October 1978 soon gave evidence of a determination to press his own claims to the full. Of all the successors of Saint Peter since the High Middle Ages, John Paul II was to bulk largest in public consciousness. Through his Polish origin, which he treated as an asset rather than a handicap, he served as a living link binding together a severed continent. Through his multiple journeys overseas he became a symbol of hope to tens of millions beyond the confines of Europe. No discussion of contemporary political culture can afford to pass over this indomitable figure—and the small but equally indomitable roster of those who opposed him.

A decade before his accession, the Church had traversed its "year of crisis." Two declarations of 1968 had preempted the future, one by narrowing vistas, the other by extending them. At the end of June the encyclical *Humanae Vitae* reaffirmed in unyielding fashion the Church's status-quo position on birth control. Overriding the majority of the commission that he himself had appointed (and which had recommended leaving the matter to the consciences of individual couples), Pope Paul VI condemned all forms of "artificial" contraception. The result was astonishment, grief, and mass disobedience. One prominent English Catholic layman went so far as to call the disarray of souls "as grave . . . as any" the Church had "faced since the Reformation."[1]

A few months later, in autumn, the Latin American bishops met at Medellín, Colombia. Following the lead of an encyclical of the previous year, *Populorum Progressio,* which had ranked the struggle between North and South, between the developed and the underdeveloped world, ahead of the conventional one between East and West, the Church fathers pledged themselves to combat social injustice. By implication they encouraged the "liberation theology" that was beginning to emerge from shantytowns and impoverished countryside alike.

Such were the key decisions with which any future pope was obliged to reckon.

A brief retrospect on the pontificate of Paul and the conclaves that followed his death may suggest how and why Cardinal Karol Wojtyła, Archbishop of Kraków, was chosen his successor. A transition pope, wedged between the two greatest of the twentieth century, Paul spent fifteen years of anguish trying to set his course. The conservative wing of the Church found him excessively tolerant of innovation; the "progressives" assailed him for his caution. Caught in the middle, trapped by his own hesitation and uncertainty, he once blurted out to a visiting papal diplomat: "Now I understand St. Peter, who came to Rome twice, the second time to be crucified."[2] (He himself had earlier served for almost thirty years in the Vatican Secretariat of State.)

On the one hand, Paul loyally carried out the legacy of his predecessor, the beloved John XXIII. He brought to a successful conclusion the Second Vatican Council. He watered down only in minor respects its declarations on Judaism, on ecumenicism, on religious liberty, on the Church in the modern world that swept away so much of Catholicism's accumulated debris and after a span of four hundred years ended the Counter Reformation. For the most part he preserved the achievements of the Council. But when it came to issues which that body had left in suspense—issues of particular urgency for West Europeans and Americans, such as the ordination of women and of married men—he drew the line (as he did on contraception). He also deplored the proliferation of experiments in worship and the boldness of postconciliar theological speculation, while refraining from firm disciplinary measures.

Western Catholics might well be puzzled. To those farther afield, however, Paul sounded more encouraging. He offered ample evidence of his sympathy for the poor—witness his advice to the bishops at Medellín. He inaugurated the practice of far-flung travel that John Paul II was so notably to amplify. He showed his concern for the faithful in Soviet-dominated Eastern Europe by launching a quiet, step-by-step *Ostpolitik* that sought to ease their lot through regularizing relations with Communist regimes. Yet eventually, as he grew older and weaker, Paul's role as "pilgrim pope" proved too much for him. After 1970 his journeys ceased; so, two years earlier, the year of *Humanae Vitae*, had his flow of encyclicals. During the last eight years of his pontificate, as he sank into weariness and pessimism, his Church existed in a state of suspended animation, anxiously awaiting a new and clearer lead.

With his death, in the first days of August 1978, clarification came, but not quite in the way those who prayed for it had intended—certainly not in the way the progressives of France, Germany, and the Low Countries, who had scored a substantial victory at the Council, had hoped. Many, perhaps most, of the cardinals believed that the time had arrived at last for a non-Italian pope. But *what sort* of non-Italian would it be?—there lay the rub. The West European progressives had no viable candidate. Moreover, they found themselves outnumbered by new cardinals from the Third World, playing for the first time a key role in a papal election and conscious of their strength as representatives of the fastest growing constituency within the Church. These too, however, coalesced around no single figure. In the conclave of late August the Italians for one last time discovered within their own ranks a candidate acceptable to all parties—a dark horse, the shy and little-known Patriarch of Venice, Albino Luciani, who took the name of John Paul I. The new pontificate lasted less than five weeks. Already suffering from a weak heart, John Paul I wore himself out with a hectic round of informal, appealing, intensely human gestures. Once again a pope lay dead; once again the cardinals, who had barely unpacked their luggage, were summoned to Rome.

The second conclave of 1978, that of October, took the leap at which its predecessor had balked. With remarkably little difficulty it chose a non-Italian. This was not the surprise. The surprise was that the assembled Church fathers elected a Pole. Yet the choice of Wojtyła was far from illogical. The Third World cardinals knew that he cared deeply about the desperate poverty of their flocks; the West European progressives had persuaded themselves that he was a "liberal."[3] He had participated in all four sessions of the Council and had become a familiar figure in Rome. The nature of that participation, however, and the clue it provided both to his thought processes and to his future course had escaped nearly everyone.

At the Council, Wojtyła had figured as alike marginal and involved. Alert and active, he nevertheless had aligned himself with no recognizable faction. The major contribution he had made was to the wording of the "pastoral constitution" on the Church in the modern world, *Gaudium et Spes* (Joy and Hope), to which he had succeeded in adding a phrase about "the transcendence of the human person." The concept recalled his earlier philosophical studies, more particularly of the German phenomenologists Edmund Husserl and Max Scheler; it encouraged the impression that Wojtyła not only was a liberal, but was an intellectual as well. Yet it was also noteworthy that he steered clear of the fine points of theology. (It subsequently emerged that he had little respect for theologians.) What people in Rome sometimes forgot— whether at the Council or at the conclaves of cardinals a decade and a half later—was that behind the helpful participant and well-endowed linguist lay a single-minded and embattled bishop, "very tough, very capable," who after first working in a stone quarry, had studied for the priesthood under harsh wartime conditions. What people also failed to notice was that for all the philosophical abstruseness and occasional opacity of his language, the new pope could be reckoned a rough-hewn man. He shared the unquestioning faith of the masses. He participated fervently in popular devotions. In a country obsessed with mariology, his cult of the Mother of God surpassed the Polish norm. (Those inclined to depth psychology could recall that he had lost his own mother at the age of nine.)

In brief, although it took a year or two for matters to become clear, the Church had acquired a stern master bent on disciplining his flock and tidying up the postconciliar confusion he saw about him. The Council itself he viewed as "an end and not a starting point"; it had "settled questions rather than opening them up."[4] Beneath the bonhomie of his public style—his enthusiasm for sport, his singing, his bantering exchanges with members of his audience (especially if they were young and Polish)—he was an man of iron determination. And he nourished a visceral distrust of what he condemned as the moral and religious slackness of the West.

No wonder that John Paul and West European or American Catholics so often talked past each other! The issue the latter regarded as of supreme importance—human liberty in matters of sex, gender, and the family and in the sphere of personal belief—seemed to the Pope "merely an irrelevant distraction." Why should these Catholics, whose rates of attendance at mass were estimated at 12–20 percent in France, perhaps 30 percent in Germany, and a little more than half in the United States, why should these folk of tepid faith, he evidently reasoned, think themselves worthy of special concern, when in his native Poland the churches were thronged to bursting? His eyes were fixed elsewhere—on the need for unity, first of all within the Catholic fold, then with the "schismatics" to the east, in lands under Soviet domination and in Russia itself. (He pursued ecumenical exchanges with the Eastern Orthodox churches more zealously than he did those with the Anglican). But to accomplish his grand design of Christian reunification, the West must "be forced to fall in behind him."[5] For that reason he cracked down on its most outspoken theologians.

At the Council theologians (more than four hundred of them!) had come into unprecedented prominence. Certain of their leading figures, who earlier had written under a cloud of Vatican disapproval, now found themselves entrusted with the task of formulating new principles for leading the Church into the future. In the euphoria engendered by Pope John's radiant goodness and the corresponding good feeling that pervaded the Council he had called, both the theologians and those who encouraged them nourished the hope that open-minded scholars would continue to play the role of intellectual vanguard. These were applauded as heroic figures, warrior-priests slaying the dragons of clerical obscurantism. They and their supporters paid insufficient heed to the danger that the spirit of the Council would dissipate in the routine application (or neglect) of its decisions at the grass-roots level of individual dioceses and parishes. By the same token, as the 1960s came to a disheartening close, the advice of theologians was less in demand than in the earlier years of the decade. By 1978, with the new papacy, the cloud that had never totally lifted was ready to redescend.

On the very same date of the following year, December 15, Edward Schillebeeckx and Hans Küng were called to order by the Roman Congregation for the Doctrine of Faith, the direct descendant of the Inquisition. For Schillebeeckx this took the form of a "conversation" on his orthodoxy, courteous but uncomfortably probing. For Küng, who refused to come to Rome for such a procedure, convinced (probably with justice) that it would be stacked against him, the verdict was delivered in writing, blunter and more categorical: a denial of teaching rights "as a Roman Catholic theologian."

This difference in treatment reflected the contrasting backgrounds and temperaments of the two men. Both came from devout families and from small, pluralingual countries (Schillebeeckx from the Flemish-speaking part of Belgium, Küng from German-speaking Switzerland); both had made their careers as professors of theology elsewhere (the former in the Netherlands, the latter in Germany); and both were steeped in contemporary secular philosophy. Beyond those similarities their lives diverged. The younger, Küng, born in 1928, seemed to relish controversy; Schillebeeckx tried to avoid it. Indeed, Küng's troubles with the Vatican had begun as early as the mid-1950s, when in his doctoral dissertation he had argued that the great Protestant theologian, his countryman Karl Barth, had taken a position basically the same as that of the Council of Trent.[6] Could the young man, the Roman defenders of orthodoxy wondered, be trying to bridge the split in Western Christianity?

Nevertheless, Küng persevered. He served as a *peritus,* or expert, at the Council. He wrote another book criticising Catholicism's authoritarian structure. The year after its publication the thunderclap of *Humanae Vitae* resounded. Küng

seized the occasion to question the entire tradition of infalli-
bility within the Church, not simply that of the Pope, which
had been invoked only once since its original enunciation by
the First Vatican Council in 1870, but of bishops and others
in authority as well. He proved beyond a doubt that the early
apostles had made no such claim; with equal cogency he drew
attention to the barrier it raised in ecumenical dialogue.[7] Yet
this book and the polemical exchanges which followed
brought down upon him the wrath of Rome.

After several years of reflection, Küng counterattacked.
While insisting that he remained a Catholic in an ecumenical
understanding of the word, based on scripture, he assaulted
head-on the reaction within the Church that was subverting
the legacy of the Council—a reaction particularly associated
with the influence of John Paul's *éminence grise,* Cardinal
Joseph Ratzinger. Unsparingly he ticked off the evidence:
denigration of Protestantism; indefinite postponement of
ecumenical understanding; a return to medieval conceptions
and usages—including the cult of Mary! The Vatican, he
added, in a characteristically pungent phrase, was swimming
"like a cork on the waves of a world-wide conservative current"; or, changing the metaphor, dissenters might no longer
"be burned at the stake," they were merely "destroyed . . . ,
psychically and professionally."[8] Yet by a curious bureaucratic twist, Küng himself escaped complete destruction.
Rome had no way of silencing him. A tenured professor at
the University of Tübingen, he was responsible only to the
government of Baden-Württemberg. An astute compromise
eventually emerged: removed from the faculty of Catholic
theology, he continued to teach in the philosophy faculty as
an ecumenical professor.

A half-generation older than Küng, Schillebeeckx was
even more the scholar and perceptibly more conservative.
(His secular studies went beyond Sartre, about whom Küng
had written, to include Heidegger, Wittgenstein, Merleau-
Ponty, Adorno, and Habermas.) He was also a less public

figure.[9] But in at least two respects he threatened conventional Catholicism more profoundly: through his critique not so much of the Church's structure and history as of its central beliefs; and through the leading position he occupied as the most respected adviser to the most deviant branch of the Church in Europe, that of the Netherlands.

In Schillebeeckx's case, the *corpus delicti* was the first volume of a vast work, published in 1974, entitled *Jesus: An Experiment in Christology*. Where Küng's prose was lively, easy to read, and comparatively brief, Schillebeeckx's was both leisurely and elliptical, replete with parentheses and qualifications. Though to a skeptic it might seem opaque, the "inquisitors" in Rome found it clear enough. For with his focus on Jesus the man, the author had sidestepped the question of his divinity and his relationship to God the Father by employing such conciliatory expressions as "the one totally filled with God's eschatological spirit." More rashly he had cast doubt on "the reality of the resurrection." And before his interrogators in Rome he dismissed as virtually unanswerable the question of whether Jesus had actually founded the Church and as "peripheral" the vexed matter of the virgin birth.[10]

Schillebeeckx, Küng, and their like constituted a special breed, an elite. As explorers of doctrinal borderlands, they recalled the "Modernists" (a grab-bag term covering a variety of tendencies suspected of heterodoxy) whom Saint Pius X had condemned in the early years of the century. But they were Modernists with a difference, sophisticated in the sense of taking care to base their arguments on precedent from the Second Vatican Council and not be caught reducing "dogmatic formulations . . . to the expression of religious feeling."[11] Moreover, they did not suffer the martyrdom of excommunication. This practice, along with that other dreaded sanction, the Index of Forbidden Books, had quietly lapsed in the wake of the Council and had not been revived. The heterodoxy of the 1970s and 1980s, theologically scrupulous and refined, threatened the Church less than the Modernism of two generations earlier. Hence the relative mildness of the sanctions imposed upon it: once the Vatican had called the theologians to order, it preferred to wash its hands of the whole business.

Although thrice subjected to ecclesiastical investigation, the last still pending at the time of his retirement from teaching in 1983, Schillebeeckx's influence within the Dutch church persisted. It may even have been enhanced. The Dutch Catholics, by reputation a stubborn lot, and a minority, although a substantial one, in their own country, had long given the Vatican cause for concern. They had produced a catechism more permissive than any comparable document, and in 1970 they had tried to include both parish priests and laymen in the process of appointment to the bishopric of Rotterdam—only to be overruled. When, in 1985, John Paul II finally visited the Netherlands, he encountered a reception unique in the annals of his travels: nearly empty streets, youthful protest demonstrations, and back talk from people quite ready to argue with him. Two issues dominated these discussions: "democracy" within the Church, and the ordination of women and married men. Among the Dutch the latter issue in particular ranked as of burning urgency, a life and death matter for the Church: "hardly any priests" were being ordained; as those authorized to officiate at mass grew older and died, pastoral workers more and more were handling everything else within the parishes. It was people like these (including women) who were filling the theological colleges, still not lacking students.[12] The conclusion seemed self-evident.

In the Netherlands, as in France or Germany, debate might rage over whether teachers such as Schillebeeckx and Küng, with their unfamiliar, nuanced formulations, were helping to keep quasi-skeptics within the fold or were "emptying the churches." In Latin America the question did not arise. Here matters were simpler, just as numbers were infinitely greater —tens of millions of the wretched of the earth. And here the theologian who aroused the Vatican's suspicions, Leonardo Boff, had taken his stand on the fundamental and unanswerable ground of Jesus' sympathy for the poor.

When in 1985 Boff in his turn was summoned to explain himself in Rome (and by the redoubtable Cardinal Ratzinger, who in the meantime had become Prefect of the Congregation for the Doctrine of Faith), the liberation theology for which he figured as the most visible spokesman had been worrying the Vatican for the better part of two decades— ever since the bishops of Latin America assembled at Medellín had given it their implicit support. Concern for the poor was not the issue. On repeated journeys to the lands where liberation theology had sprung up, John Paul II left no doubt about his own compassion and distress. It was rather that the priests and laymen in question worked in community groups without formal ecclesiastical supervision, that they distrusted the Church's hierarchical organization (which Boff had dared compare to the Communist Party of the Soviet Union), that their language smacked of Marxism, and that some of them maintained ties with guerrillas and insurrectionists. Not all the Latin American bishops saw virtue in liberation theology. But a number of the most prominent did, including two cardinals from Boff's own country, Brazil, who in an unprecedented gesture of solidarity accompanied him to his hearing (or "conversation" or "colloquy," or better, "interrogation") in Rome. To no avail: on May 1 Boff was condemned to a year of silence, that is, a year without writing or speaking in public, a verdict he scrupulously obeyed.

While the Brazilian priest was holding his tongue, the Pope evidently began to have second thoughts. Unlike Küng and Schillebeeckx, Boff had a mass movement behind him, and in a country whose Catholics outnumbered those of any other nation on earth. Before the penitential year had elapsed, signs of relenting began to emanate from the Vatican. First John Paul met for three days with more than twenty of Brazil's senior bishops. Second it became known that the Vatican was preparing a new document on liberation theology. Finally, as an "Easter present," the ban on Boff's speaking and writing was lifted one month early.

What had happened? The simple answer seems to be that the Pope and his advisers had gradually come to realize that the questions raised by liberation theology were not confined to Latin America (although this was important enough in itself). They were worldwide: they were relevant wherever the masses lived oppressed by despotic or oligarchic rule and by the callousness of the rich and the powerful. Hence the relatively understanding tone of the new "Instruction on Christian Liberty and Liberation." As Boff himself had expressed it, the credibility of the Church throughout the Third World was at stake.[13]

The compromise on liberation theology could have prompted a more inclusive trade-off: rigidity on dogma balanced by permissiveness in matters involving the secular world. Only the West—and only the learned and/or devout within it—cared profoundly about dogma. The majority shrugged their shoulders and kept their understanding of the faith to themselves. They applauded the Pope as a human being and dozed off when he turned to issues of theology. As a French observer put it, they preferred "the singer to the words."[14] In common with that other "great communicator," Ronald Reagan, John Paul's communications aroused enthusiasm through their very lack of substance. Outside the Netherlands he ran little risk of a mass exodus of the faithful when he took steps to curb his scholarly antagonists. Yet the same mass of the Western faithful saw no harm in women or married men serving as priests and resented ecclesiastical snooping into their contraceptive practices. Why couldn't the Pope leave them alone? How would that have threatened the fundamentals of Catholicism? So they wondered. This John Paul II evidently failed to acknowledge: the trade-off failed to occur.

We can begin to understand why if we think of the Pope too as a rebel, a rebel against the evil he saw in the soulless world of contemporary urban existence. Consider his a voice crying in the wilderness, one whose rebelliousness took forms difficult for the Western mind to comprehend: a stern, self-denying notion of the priesthood; a corresponding notion of a special role for women, modeled on the shining example of Mary; a revulsion from tampering with procreation. To appreciate John Paul II in his own dimension it was necessary to visualize him in his native land.

His triumphal return to Poland in June 1979, eight months after his elevation to the papacy, surpassed any other such experience in the history of modern Europe. Something approaching twelve million people—a third of the country's population—saw him. The government's writ ceased to run. The Church controlled the streets and squares of the cities through which the Pope passed. Policing was scarcely required: the crowds disciplined themselves; the atmosphere was of joyous attentiveness, with no trace of religious hysteria. Among his own people and speaking the language he loved, John Paul II became once again the homespun Karol Wojtyła. He sang along with his hearers, sometimes, in his resonant bass, even starting the singing. The vast majority of those who heard him were Catholics, as went without saying in Poland. But skeptics too were touched, much to their own surprise. (On his departure back to Rome, the Pope impulsively embraced President Jabłoński, who had come to see him off. The atheist, Communist head of state responded by bending to kiss John Paul's hands.) "The word 'miracle' was on the lips of both churchgoing old women and intellectuals."

In another fourteen months a second miracle would occur. Once a backwater, Poland had suddenly become "the most interesting country in the world."[15]

SIX

The Sixteen Months of Solidarity

The rise and fall of Solidarity in Poland did not lack chroniclers. Of all the era's rebellions it became the best documented and the one that most graphically caught the public imagination—just as it was the first in history to be played out under the scrutiny of television cameras. It was also the movement of liberation that brought the greatest enrichment to Europe's political culture. Since its major vicissitudes have been indelibly etched on the historical consciousness of Europeans and Americans alike, to retrace them would be a pointless exercise. The point, rather, is to demonstrate how Solidarity was plagued by an uncertainty that lingered on long after its official dissolution. Its *moral* lesson shone bright and clear: its strategic lesson remained clouded and the subject of passionate debate.

Among its origins three require elaboration: the Polish version of the Europe-wide rumblings of 1968, the preparatory work of intellectuals, the role of the Catholic church.

In Poland the crucial spring of 1968 broke the last threads of understanding between writers and cultural leaders, on the one hand, and the government and Communist party, on the other. The year before, Israel's Six-Day War had provided a pretext for unleashing a strident anti-Semitic campaign, a campaign which drove into exile the greater part of Poland's pathetically small Jewish remnant, among them a distinguished contingent of intellectuals. The following March the police launched an attack on a peaceful student meeting at Warsaw University, succeeded by a wave of purges and arrests. Finally the Soviet snuffing out of Dubček's liberal reforms in Czechoslovakia—and shame at Polish participation in the invasion—ended the last lingering hopes for a "revision" of the Communist system. From this succession of events, Poland's intellectuals drew the conclusion that they were now on their own, that they and they alone could lay the basis for a pluralist society in which not only Catholicsm, but Judaism as well, would receive the respect they deserved.

The fruit of this rethinking was the association called KOR, an acronym for Workers' Defense Committee. Founded in the summer of 1976 in the wake of severe repression in the factories, it initially aimed to give material and legal assistance to workers who had lost their jobs or were facing trial. Soon, however, it broadened its scope to include the defense of anyone whose civil rights were threatened, plus publishing the facts on beatings, acts of intimidation, and the like that the authorities tried to cover up. It also warmly supported the Flying University, a loosely knit series of lecture courses on forbidden or controversial topics held in private homes and occasionally in Church facilities. (Among the ecclesiastics providing such quarters was the Cardinal-Archbishop of Kraków, Karol Wojtyła, soon to be elevated to the papacy.) In short, KOR linked intellectuals and workers in unprecedented fashion by serving as a clearinghouse for protests of all sorts against official callousness and disregard of the law. It even reached beyond Poland's borders to maintain a tenuous contact with Soviet dissidents such as Andrei D. Sakharov and with the gallant band of post-1968 holdouts for freedom in Czechoslovakia who called themselves Charter '77.

The most novel thing about KOR was its transparent openness. Acting on the principle that one should behave "as if" Poland were already a free society, it made no secret of its membership, whose addresses and telephone numbers it announced, and it tried to keep its activities within the confines of a meticulously defined legality. It scorned the usual paraphernalia of chairmen, bylaws, and membership fees; those who emerged as leaders did so simply by working harder and more effectively than the others. Its ethos, defined for the most part by implication and example, stressed matter-of-factness and scrupulous honesty, nonviolence and forbearance, plus reluctance to sit in judgment. Much of this echoed the basic Christian tenet of charity, and KOR's members, largely unbelievers, soon found themselves pursuing their goals in harmony with Catholic colleagues. Such was the "voice in the wilderness," the indispensable prelude to what followed, which despite hounding and imprisonment, had kept its integrity untarnished when it dissolved itself into its mighty successor, Solidarity.[1]

"It is hard to conceive of Solidarity without the Polish Pope": so wrote its best-informed and most spirited chronicler.[2] In retrospect, John Paul's visit appeared the catalyst or dress rehearsal for the tumultuous events that occurred fourteen months later. Such was the most visible and dramatic expression of the third element in Solidarity's origins: the mounting self-confidence of the Church in extending help and comfort to those who had fallen foul of the regime. Within Poland's redrawn boundaries of 1945 the population could be reckoned 90 percent Catholic; few had followed their Communist rulers' atheist injunctions; here, almost alone in Europe, the working class held to its traditional faith. And they could look for guidance to the aged and indomitable primate, Cardinal Stefan Wyszyński, who had resisted both prison and official blandishments. As the 1970s advanced, the practice of religion increased alongside the growing sympathy of the cultural leadership for Christian values. In the end there emerged "a tacit alliance of the intellectual opposition, the Church, and the workers."[3]

Thus it was that when, in mid-August 1980, at the Lenin Shipyard in Gdańsk, a discharged electrician, Lech Wałęsa, climbed up on a bulky piece of machinery and with infectious buoyancy declared an occupation-strike, all the elements were in place for a sympathetic response nationwide. Not only in Gdańsk (the former Danzig) were workers angry; throughout the country ordinary people were aghast at the insensitivity of a government that without warning had reduced the subsidies which held down food prices and at the rise in the cost of such products as sugar and meat that followed. Economic protest triggered the explosion. Below it lay a profound aversion to the regime under which Poland was languishing and a longing, mostly inarticulate, for a more human and humane society.

It was characteristic of Wałęsa and his coworkers that their first six demands not only specified the right to form trade unions authorized to strike and free from Communist party control, but also called for the reinstatement "of students . . . excluded from institutions of higher education because of their opinions," the liberation of "all political prisoners," an end to "measures against independent publications," and "access to the mass media for representatives of all religions." Only after the government had substantially agreed to these points, did the strike come to an end.

The foundation of Solidarity the following month, with Wałęsa at its head, formalized the mix of ethical, civic, and trade-union provisions. A year later, in a program hammered out at an ultraparticipatory and sometimes unruly congress, the same principles prevailed once again—unashamedly eclectic in their debt to both socialism and Christianity, to both liberal democracy and conservatism, but ruggedly coherent in spirit.[4] By that time Solidarity had enrolled nine and a half million members and could claim to speak for the vast majority of Poles. It had also scored a few tangible victories, notably the right of peasants to form "associations" as modest versions of the giant trade union and a censorship law which specified at last the limits to official supervision.

In the Gdańsk Agreement, Wałęsa and his associates had recognized "the leading role" of the Communist party "in the state" and "the existing system of international alliances." The words in the state need underlining. They held the key to the realism (or sophistication?) of Solidarity's leadership and to the residues of illusion that went along with it. These leaders were far from the romantic Poles of national legend or foreign scorn. They knew that it would be folly to challenge the structure of the state or its dependence on the Soviet Union. (One of the very few matters on which government and opposition agreed was the absolute imperative of avoiding intervention on the Budapest or Prague model.) Hence the latter conceived a revolution which would be "self-limiting," a revolution "of the soul" without violence or bloodshed and one which would renounce the customary goal of taking over the state. The expression in the state also implied that Poland's rulers should stick to their own business of governing, narrowly defined: they would not meddle with labor, education, or religion. On this understanding, on the understanding that the authoritarian state would little by little reduce itself to a hollow shell, Solidarity and its supporters—the overwhelming mass of the Poles—aimed to build up within the shell the institutions of a free society, a gentle, a pluralist society, above all, a society in which men and women could live and work *in dignity*. Perhaps (and this is to extrapolate wildly from what Solidarity's leaders actually said), perhaps years down the road the irremediably corrupted state itself, in the hallowed Marxist phrase, would wither away.

This astounding mélange of common sense and vision was a unique and heartening contribution to the stale routines of Europe's political culture. Would Poland's rulers abide by so one-side a concept of coexistence? The answer came with brutal suddenness, on December 13, 1981, with the imposition of martial law and the dissolution of Solidarity. The opposition was caught by surprise; "virtually no one believed in the possibility of an armed coup d'état." What can explain so disastrous a miscalculation?

"Solidarity lacked familiarity with its enemy and the enemy's methods . . . It was a colossus with legs of steel and hands of clay; it was powerful among factory crews but powerless at the negotiating table. Across the table sat a partner who could not be truthful, run an economy, or keep its word—who could do but one thing: break up" the newly formed social consensus.[5] Such was the wry retrospective judgment of one of Solidarity's clearest heads, Adam Michnik. He might have added that he and Wałęsa and the rest had failed to reckon with the fact that among all the disintegrating elements of state and party, the army alone remained intact, and under a chief who combined machinelike efficiency with devotion to his concept of the public good.

Solidarity's leaders exuded good will—but, along with it, volubility and disputatiousness. Wałęsa's primacy was never secure; he always had to contend with hotheads and jealous rivals. Small, outwardly unimpressive, his face adorned by a comic moustache—"part king, part holy fool," as one sympathetic witness characterized him—he needed to play to the gallery to maintain his shaky authority.[6] Most of the time he seemed to relish the act; most of the time his cajolery brought his hearers round. But now and then when the going got too rough, he would simply absent himself from a meeting until passions cooled. Astute if unlettered, profoundly religious, he would have made a great ecclesiastic. Here was a man who for all his ebullience was groping his way through a minefield, forever in doubt about what the next step might encounter.

To compensate for their lack of formal education, Wałęsa and the other authentic workers in the movement could call on those they referred to as experts—veterans of KOR who often were far from expert in the fields (economics primarily) on which they were supposed to advise, but who could at least offer counsels of prudence. Although *sui generis,* Michnik may stand for the rest. Still in his mid-thirties, he had imbibed his ideals not from the Church but from parents who "were Polish Communists of Jewish origin" and who had taught him to take socialism seriously—hence an inevitable rupture with a regime that had reduced it to a sham.[7] As an activist student working for a degree in history, he had undergone the second of his many imprisonments after the 1968 protests; he had lectured for the Flying University; he had performed skilled labor and come to know workers at close quarters. Like his friend Wałęsa, Michnik enjoyed life to the full—there was nothing ascetic about either man—and could address crowds with ease and persuasiveness. One day at the height of Solidarity's influence he deployed this talent to rescue a policeman from an angry mob. His antagonists in the official establishment would doubtless have found his action incomprehensible. Spontaneous human sympathy was not their forte.

No one could have accused of such frailty the man who took over the premiership in February 1981 and eight months later reinforced his authority by becoming head of the Communist Party. "A flat inscrutable face. Thin lips clamped shut above a sharp, clean jaw. The small head set bolt upright, as if fixed to the spine by a steel pin. A trim figure looking fragile inside the heavy uniform ... Eyes ... hidden behind large rectangular dark glasses" giving "the whole an expression of almost inhuman blankness—faintly menacing."[8] Although General Wojciech Jaruzelski had been minister of defense for twelve years, and a member of the Politburo for a decade, he had remained a shadowy, mysterious figure until he reached the very top. From then on he was constantly in the news. But the mystery could not so easily be dispelled. Even American judgments on him varied erratically: the secretary of defense dismissed him as a "Soviet general in Polish uniform"; an experienced and respected journalist who had heard him speak at a meeting of his Warsaw Pact peers found his the only "refreshing, . . . candid voice" in a "flood of wooden words."[9] Actually the solution to the riddle was quite simple: Jaruzelski was both a loyal Muscovite Communist and a Polish patriot.

His biography was as eccentric as Michnik's. The offspring of Polish gentry with an elite Jesuit education, as a teenager, alongside so many others of his class, he had been deported east when the Soviet Union joined Nazi Germany in partitioning his country. Deep inside Russia he had undergone the Communist indoctrination reserved for those not summarily shot. In his case the ideological drilling succeeded. He became a steadfast, even ruthless Soviet-style warrior. By 1956 he was Poland's youngest general; twelve years later he was supervising his country's participation in the march on Prague. People said that in 1970 he had refused to fire on striking workers. In a ruling caste almost universally tainted by material self-seeking, he enjoyed a reputation for incorruptibility, even asceticism. From such bits and pieces of life history, an integrated, if atypical, figure emerges. But Jaruzelski himself would never have provided the clue. One suspects that he had gone through so desperately painful an adolescence that he had learned the hard way to veil his emotions (hence the dark glasses?) and to confront the world with icy impassivity.

These three were all personalities of major dimensions. Had they been able to play out their parts on a larger stage, they could have become world figures. The same could not be said of a fourth actor, Mieczysław F. Rakowski, who, however, needs to join the cast, since as vice-premier in charge of relations with Solidarity he served as Jaruzelski's close coworker and spokesman.

A sharper contrast in origins and character than that between Rakowski and his chief could scarcely be imagined. Of peasant stock, mentally agile, and a charmer when charm was required, the vice-premier had mounted the ranks of the Communist Party—still more, had made himself distinctive—through the gift of divining precisely the measure of deviation from orthodoxy he could get away with. He figured as the party's best journalist and best ambassador-at-large to the West, where people considered him a reformer—which to an extent he was. For his own part, he thought of himself as a "man of the middle," a congenital arbiter.[10]

The deal he offered Solidarity he referred to as "partnership." But what he meant by the word was at least as unequal as his "partners'" aspirations for the future. In Rakowski's interpretation it signified a power-sharing in which the party would call the tune. He depicted himself as baffled by Solidarity's reluctance to go along, by its obstruction and its obtuseness. He accused his opposite numbers of failure to recognize the danger of economic collapse (which was only too real), of loss of national sovereignty (doubtless a code expression for Soviet intervention), and of being pushed by their own "extremists" to come forward as a frankly political force or an alternative government.[11]

In this last charge lay the nub of the matter. At the time many observers, even in the West, argued that Solidarity had gone too far, had brought fate down on its own head by violating its self-limiting principle. Subsequently the view prevailed that Jaruzelski had prepared for military action *before* Solidarity gave him grounds to resort to force. Are these two views in any sense reconcilable? To answer that question we must proceed in two stages: first, a timetable of events; second, a definition, both nuanced and precise, of what Solidarity was demanding in the last months of its legal existence.

On the matter of timetable, the evidence, although indirect, seems conclusive. Jaruzelski's "shift . . . from the political to the military option must . . . be placed between late July and late September" of 1981—that is, at the very latest, a week before October 7, when the "second round" of Solidarity's congress voted its program and adjourned. So much is clear. But four weeks earlier, during its "first round," the congress had passed a resolution on workers' self-government which so alarmed the Soviet leadership that it ordered its ambassador to interevene.[12] Did this trigger the preparations for martial law? Unlikely: in the inverval between the two rounds Wałęsa had negotiated a compromise that apparently satisfied the General and Rakowski. Events were moving swiftly: the timetable of one side's actions criss-crossed with that of the other. Overall, however, the judgment stands: Poland's ruler was proceeding independently of what Solidarity was doing or had done.

What precisely, had it done? In its program for a "self-governing republic," it had not gone beyond demanding free local elections. Not until December 12, the day before the imposition of martial law, did the chief wildcat among Solidarity's spokesmen explicitly propose equally free elections for the national parliament. What the program voted two months earlier had stressed was grass-roots initiative and decentralization.[13] Did that in itself constitute a threat to the state?

The answer depends on what one means by "going too far." Solidarity's "official" statements tried to reassure a government at bay and a tottering Communist Party. The actions of its component parts increasingly did not. As the months wore on, both factionalism—personal challenges to Wałęsa's leadership—and radical rhetoric became more pronounced. In Michnik's words, Solidarity "allowed itself to be provoked into fights over minor issues . . . ; it was often disorderly and incompetent . . . The sudden politicization of hundreds of thousands of people who used to be passive, and thus were not familiar with political life, produced an . . . explosive . . . combination of populism and nationalism richly decorated with religious symbols"—a tendency springing "from poverty, hysteria, and demagoguery, . . . whose screaming drowned out every proposed strategic initiative." With the detachment afforded by prison life, Solidarity's former "expert" could see very well where and how things had gone wrong. His letter, smuggled out of jail, was intended both as a critique of the past and an admonition for the future. In effect, he was telling his comrades that in their day-to-day conduct of the struggle for a free Poland they had "gone too far."

What Michnik would not admit was that local irresponsibility and the sporadic chaos that Rakowski lamented justified Jaruzelski's armed response. The most he would grant was that Solidarity lacked "a well-defined concept of coexistence with the communist regime."[14] With this he reached the crux of the entire retrospective debate. In the end Solidarity succumbed to an uncertainty present from the very start. Its self-limiting principle could be (and was) interpreted either narrowly or broadly as the case arose. Such a principle demanded heroic self-discipline on the part of its adherents. And this was too much to expect from people intoxicated by the novel experience of freedom. Yet when all the foregoing has been said, a positive conclusion cannot fail to emerge: of the era's movements of political renewal, Solidarity proved the most inventive, the broadest-based, and the most resilient in the face of catastrophe.

That catastrophe, under the banner of martial law, took the form of systematically destroying or scattering Solidarity's strongholds. Of the once-mighty union's leaders, some resisted, some went underground, the majority eventually landed up in prison; Wałęsa himself "enjoyed" the privilege of comfortable special detention. In all, only twenty-eight people lost their lives, a tribute to Jaruzelski's resolve to keep bloodshed to a minimum.[15] In the same spirit, in December 1982 and July 1983 the General proclaimed a two-stage lifting of the rigors of martial law. But what one hand gave, the other took back: new restrictions followed. The same was true of a series of amnesties and reimprisonments. Not until September 1986 did Jaruzelski feel sufficiently secure to liberate his remaining enemies.

In the intervening half decade Solidarity had refused to die; it had lived on as a clandestine network and a golden memory. That fact in itself sufficed to belie the notion that the General had brought a crushed and sullen people to heel. In curbing dissent, he had in fact proceeded cautiously: he did not attempt a thoroughgoing "normalization" on the post-1968 Czech model. While bearing down on urban workers and intellectuals, he reassured the landholding peasantry (estimated at 85 percent of the total) by giving them a constitutional guarantee of permanent tenure. For the most part, he kept his hands off the Church. In brief, he settled for a Poland which might be Communist in its outward trappings, its foreign policy, and its apparatus of repression, but which could no longer be called such in the essentials of life behind the ideological facade.

This was what Michnik called the real latter-day "miracle on the Vistula"—harking back to 1920 and the glorious repulse of the newly created Red Army—the ability of the Poles to cling to their "spiritual freedom" in dangerous and depressing circumstances.[16] Above all, they had learned to cling to their Church—"the only Polish institution to have been strengthened both by the rise of Solidarity *and* by" its suppression. A year and a half after that event Pope John Paul II paid another visit to his native land. This time, understandably, his reception could not be as joyous as it had been in 1979. But the response to his presence and his words was equally profound, perhaps even more so, in view of the spectacular passage from jubilation to dejection that had occurred in the four years between the two journeys. At Poland's holiest spot, the monastery of Jasna Góra, the "pilgrim" from Rome addressed half a million fellow Catholics, who hung on his every word with intense, silent emotion. Enjoining them "to erect a barricade against demoralisation," he quietly dropped into his homily the magic word "solidarity."[17]

His hearers knew that they were in for a long, long march indeed. As a starting point they could reckon what they had preserved: an independent intellectual life without parallel in the whole of eastern Europe. At the mid-decade a British journalist estimated at fifty to sixty thousand the number of Poles engaged in underground activities of one or another variety; at one thousand the number of clandestine bulletins circulating; at fifty the monthly total of books illegally published.[18] The substructure for future protest was intact and likely to remain so. But what tangible hope could the Poles build upon it?

The opposition, whether clandestine or tolerated, held one trump card in its emaciated hand: the reluctance, amounting almost to phobia, of the Soviet leadership to intervene by military might in Poland's affairs. This was the nightmare, "the worst," which Jaruzelski had forestalled, thereby earning the (for once) heartfelt gratitude of his sponsors to the east. The card, however, needed to be played with consummate skill. The Poles' longing for freedom needed to be kept in balance with recognition of their uniquely exposed geopolitical situation. Of all the dependent peoples, they were the one to whose continued dependence the Soviet Union gave the highest priority in its security calculations. Thus the Polish opposition was obliged to envisage a perpetual game of squaring the circle. As Michnik wrote in 1980, in words that still held true a half decade later, the best that could be hoped for was "a hybrid system," authoritarian without, democratic within, which "by its very nature . . . would . . . be provisional." "Any attempt," he specified, "to govern counter to the people's will" was "bound to lead to disaster; . . . any attempt to overthrow communist rule in Poland" threatened "the interests of the USSR." Such was the reality that "must be understood."[19]

92

On the fifth anniversary of the Gdańsk Agreement, Bronisław Geremek, a friend and professional colleague of Michnik, inserted a further and perhaps conclusive reflection into
the puzzle. Poland could not emerge from the twilight of the
precarious and the provisional, he implied, unless and until
the international community as a whole began to pursue
hitherto "unexplored possibilities" Europe-wide in scope.
But such an exploration could not be launched under pressure from or "for the profit" of the United States; this the
Soviet Union would "never accept." A reduction of tension
between the superpowers—that and that alone—would permit the allies on both sides of the great divide to develop their
own policy, to find their way toward "a European solution"
in which Poland could achieve "a different political status."[20]

What that solution and that status might be necessarily
remained nebulous. At the very least they would offer a
chance for the Poles' return to the cultural community of the
West, where they believed they belonged, and their expulsion
from which they resented as by no means the lightest of the
burdens that Soviet overlordship had imposed upon them.
Once more, as with Milan Kundera, we hear the note of
longing for the reunification of a sundered continent.

SEVEN

The Frustration of Soviet Dissent

The men and women who in the Soviet Union itself followed the stony path of dissent faced dangers and disappointments far beyond those encountered by their Polish peers. Dissent in Poland could count on the backing of a homogeneous people—overt support from the working class and tacit sympathy among the peasants. In the Soviet Union it was the reverse: the dissidents formed a beleaguered band drawn largely from the intelligentsia and cut off from the mass of the population by a wall of mutual incomprehension. Polish dissent drew on patriotic traditions reaching back nearly two centuries; Soviet dissent smacked of treason.

Such held true for the dominant ethnic Russians. Among the minor Soviet peoples—more particularly among Ukrainians, Georgians, and Armenians, Lithuanians, Latvians, and Estonians—patriotic resistance here and there united intellectuals and ordinary folk in a common hatred of Russian overlordship. But movements of this sort languished in obscurity; it was not they that inspired interest and sympathy in the West. Nor was it religious protest, whether Eastern Orthodox or evangelical Protestant; only the pleas of the Jews found support abroad. Yet even Jewish protest fastened almost exclusively on the issue of emigration; such single-mindedness often sounded like indifference to the wider question of arbitrary rule at home. By contrast, the

94

greatest of the Russian dissidents tried to see beyond the plight of their own people to that of the other Soviet nationalities and of humanity as a whole. Their numbers, their eminence, the fact that only they wrote in a major international language, dictate a focus on their struggles and their frustration.

A final distinction: the overwhelming majority of Poles rejected both Marxist ideology and Communist practice; their faith and fervor they vested in their church. A similar majority of Russians lacked any form of religion; Communist doctrine had to suffice. Not that it aroused anything approaching the devotion which Catholicism inspired among the Poles. But it had been in power for two generations; most people had been born under its auspices; as an economic system, at the very least, it was taken for granted, even approved. These were the givens with which Soviet dissent had to reckon; it was in no position to envisage a new type of society such as dazzled the imaginations of Solidarity's activists. It was obliged to pursue a simpler goal: a liberal ideal stripped to its essentials of basic human rights. With such a goal—and with it alone, "because of its neutrality with respect to religion, politics, and ethnic origin"—could links be forged among scattered and disparate movements in a vast and heterogeneous population.[1]

Where should the story begin? At the very earliest with Nikita Khrushchev's 1956 speech to the Twentieth Congress of the Soviet Union's Communist Party and his (selective) exposure of the "crimes of the Stalin era." With it, and with the liberation of literally millions from forced labor in the frozen north, there began a "thaw" whose dimensions remained uncertain and which never reached the flood for which so many had hoped. Yet one novelty proved undeniable: for the first time since the 1920s a visible opposition had raised its head.

Beyond that, a set of technological and social changes had occurred that made a full return to Stalinism unfeasible. In

95

the 1960s a "communications explosion" altered long-established living patterns: the number of radios doubled, the number of television sets increased tenfold; by 1970 tape recorders had come into general circulation.[2] Where the educated Soviet citizen had once heard the news from loudspeakers blaring in public, he could now listen in the privacy of his home and discuss with trusted friends how to interpret the official version. Foreign broadcasts could also contribute to this process. More people were able to afford short-wave sets, and the jamming of messages from the West was becoming less frequent. Permission to travel abroad—naturally under escort—was likewise becoming more widely available. Such changes taken together enormously increased the stock of information at the disposal of those sufficiently clever or sufficiently motivated to take advantage of them. And it was these who learned the art of ideological bilingualism, how to speak one language—the official language—on the job, and the other—the language of independent thought (now tolerated, so long as it was quiet)—with those of similarly inquiring mind.[3]

In these new conditions, an intelligentsia reemerged. The designation, coined in nineteenth-century Russia for the "politically aware, critically thinking segment of the educated class," took on contemporary relevance, and that segment began to separate off into a distinct social stratum, as opposed to those who earlier had been mere "mental technicians" or barely tolerated, if indispensable, survivors from the old regime. This new segment tended to live closely packed together—in special blocks of cooperative apartments in Moscow or in isolated research towns created de novo from on high. The isolation of these "science cities"—in one major case, deep in Siberia—sprang from the authorities' concern, both ideological and security-conscious, to protect the population at large from the contamination of critical thought. But warding off one danger produced another: the new research centers, by the very fact that so much talent was concentrated in them, became intellectual hothouses in which lively minds with few outside distractions could focus intensely on a few key issues or events. Word of mouth traveled fast from one such oasis to another—and eventually to the Soviet world outside.[4]

Nor was it possible (the numbers were too vast) to restrict contact between ordinary citizens and those released from labor camps. These latter-day Lazaruses had stories to tell, stories which could shock their listeners into sudden awareness of the gruesome underpinnings of Soviet society. Beyond that, they could teach those bold enough to listen the well-tried techniques of underground contact. Gradually a conspiratorial or semi-conspiratorial network also began to emerge, a network whose ramifications paralleled and opposed that of the Gulag itself.[5] The chief technique was *samizdat,* "the self-publication" of writings the censorship had refused (or doubtless would refuse) to pass. Most of such work circulated in typescript, with a maximum number of carbon copies, often barely legible. Copies multiplied as dozens of exhausted, devoted women labored night after night to sustain the flow; eventually a few chosen spirits amassed whole libraries of such forbidden fare. Through that very process the original authors lost control of their own productions. Yet theirs remained the ultimate responsibility and the ultimate peril from official wrath. As one author succinctly portrayed the all-too-frequent succession of events: "I write it myself, censor it myself, print and disseminate it myself, and then I do time in prison for it myself."[6]

We are already deep into the first phase of dissent, the literary phase, the phase of hope and illusion. In the late 1950s, it began to be possible to publish under official auspices poems and novels that depicted Soviet society with an honesty unfettered by the clichés of "socialist realism." Of course one had to take precautions; one could not tell *everything;* and one had to rely on one's publisher to vet the work with an experienced eye. The past master of such fencing with the censorship was Alexander Tvardovsky, editor of the chief independent literary review, *Novy Mir* (New World), who combined courage and astuteness in equal measure. It was he who published the novel that sounded the first salvo of the newly discovered, precarious quasi-freedom: Vladimir Dudintsev's *Not by Bread Alone,* the account of an innovative engineer's ultimately successful struggle against the cynicism, the corruption, of entrenched bureaucrats and academicians. Dudintsev's novel inaugurated a cautious skirmish, with criticism still muted, and the great dissidents of the late 1960s and 1970s still holding their fire. Its climax (and end), again under Tvardovsky's aegis, and only through the personal intervention of Khrushchev himself, came in 1962 with the publication of Alexander Solzhenitsyn's *One Day in the Life of Ivan Denisovich.*

Two years later Khrushchev fell from power, and two years after that the chill redescended. Andrei Sinyavsky and Yuli Daniel, a pair of unorthodox writers who under assumed names had resorted to the still newer device of *tamizdat* (or publication "there," that is, in the West) were brought to trial and sentenced to strict-regimen labor camps. The furor abroad unleashed by so harsh a verdict evidently gave the regime second thoughts; subsequently it did not arrest writers simply for the "crime" of tamizdat, and the practice became increasingly common.[7] But mere unauthorized publication was one thing, the material published quite another. On the latter the authorities left no room for doubt. The case of Sinyavsky and Daniel marked a watershed. From 1966 on those who ventured into the treacherous currents of samizdat or tamizdat or even made futile attempts to wiggle or cajole their way past the censor knew that they were putting themselves in grave peril.

Something, however, had been gained. The independent writers, the fledgling dissidents, who once had lived cut off from one another and ignorant of each other's efforts, had learned to know and to respect the names that counted. In

Solzhenitsyn's retrospective view a decade later, "During the seven years of our frail and pale freedom some things did nevertheless emerge, . . . and one swimmer in the dawn-lit ocean . . . spied another head and cried out in a wheezy voice to him."[8]

Solzhenitsyn epitomized the transition from literary originality to militant dissent. Still an obscure provincial schoolteacher when *Ivan Denisovich* catapulted him to fame, he had taken decades to grope his way toward the ideological position which he had by then reached. It took him even longer to disclose the full dimensions of the task on which he had embarked, and another few years for his readers (who could hardly believe the evidence of what they were reading) to grasp and to digest the message of a man whose hubris left them astounded.

From the start everything about Solzhenitsyn seemed out of focus; from the start no preestablished categories fitted the "chaos and suffering" in which his life began and which were to brand it indelibly thereafter.[9] Born at the end of 1918, he never knew the father who had died a half-year before, in a hunting accident, after surviving the rigors of First World War service. The torment and confusion of the Civil War in the south set the tone for the boy's first years. Buffeted from one place to another by events which passed her understanding, his widowed mother eventually settled into a small-town life of genteel poverty. Of prosperous peasant stock, she and her only child hovered in marginality, ethnically part Russian and part Ukrainian, socially just within the educated class to which her husband had risen. In his childhood and youth Solzhenitsyn was obliged to sort out conflicting loyalties: he aspired toward both literature and physics—the latter becoming his university subject of study. The first of these enthusiasms reflected the fascination exerted on him by an aunt who steeped his mind in the richly tinted lore of Russia's past; the second bore the mark of the "scientific" determinism, the steely dogmas of the Marxism he had learned at school. But even his ideological allegiance he espoused with a difference.

"Back to Leninism and to Leninist norms": with this slogan he and his best friend at the university encapsulated their secret contempt for Stalin and their unbounded admiration for his predecessor. It was also what brought Solzhenitsyn to grief. In the final months of the Second World War the police intercepted his correspondence with that same friend. As the Red Army was smashing into East Prussia—in the ruthless fury which Michel Tournier evoked from the other side and which inspired Solzhenitsyn's first poetry (while turning his stomach)—the twice-decorated artillery captain found himself subjected to the dreadful humiliation of being stripped of his rank (of which he was unashamedly proud) and hustled off to jail. His first reaction was incredulity; and such for a long time it remained.

Bits and pieces—indeed the greater part—of what happened thereafter were to figure, frequently in transparent disguise, in Solzhenitsyn's major writings. The outlines of his decade and more of detention are by now familiar: his privileged scientific labor at a secret research center; his subsequent hard labor as a bricklayer in a regular camp; his bout with cancer; his three years of internal exile as a schoolteacher in Kazakhstan, where he was at last able to devote himself to writing, and from which he was liberated two months after Khrushchev announced the leap into de-Stalinization. The story reads like a grim variety of *Bildungsroman,* a protracted education which the protagonist was eventually to view in religious terms as a step-by-step ascent to authentic understanding. And unless we, his readers, appreciate this, we cannot possibly grasp the full force of his subsequent quixotic outburst: "*Bless you, prison,* for having been in my life!"[10]

Of all these stages toward a higher vision, the stay at the

research center, familiarly called *sharashka,* ranked as the "most rewarding . . . ; it was the richest and most varied cultural environment he was ever to find himself in." In the range of conversation and debate it furnished, it was magical, "the freest in the whole of the Soviet Union . . . And it provided the material for his . . . best novel: *The First Circle.*"[11]

The "magic circle" might figure as a successor to Thomas Mann's *The Magic Mountain.* As in Mann's Swiss sanatorium, two preceptors (in this case real rather than invented) struggled for a young man's soul, with victory seesawing back and forth between them. Neither, however, stood for the Western liberal-democratic values that later inspired the core of Soviet dissent. One, despite the suffering the regime inflicted on him, remained a Bolshevik true believer. The other unswervingly held to old Russian values, Orthodox religion and all. In the end, his Leninism long since discarded, Solzhenitsyn opted for the latter (and for the memory of his aunt!). The process had been gradual: it had reached fulfillment four years after he had left the sharashka and found himself entering a church and giving "thanks to God for his recovery" from cancer.[12] The year following, 1955, in belated recognition that his true gift lay with prose rather than poetry, he began the novel which, after more than another decade had passed, took rank as his masterpiece.

Meantime *Ivan Denisovich* had thrown his readers off the track. Purged of its more unpalatable passages by Tvardovsky's affectionately wielded blue pencil, the little book and its prisoner-bricklayer protagonist had "touched" Khrushchev, who particularly liked how Ivan measured out his mortar. Along with their chief, it had entranced hundreds of thousands of ordinary Russians. Few saw through its deceptive simplicity; few appreciated the skill with which Solzhenitsyn had deployed a cast of supporting characters from widely varied backgrounds who together created "a panorama of Soviet life and Soviet history, a universalized portrait of suffering and oppression." But most understood enough

101

to experience an "enormous sense of spiritual and psychological relief" that a tiny but infinitely precious fragment of the truth had at last and so compellingly been told. Those not ready for harsher fare could take comfort in the ending: Ivan's day "had been almost happy." And along with them, the official *Izvestia* went so far as to declare his creator "a true helper of the Party."[13]

On the strength of so profound a misapprehension Solzhenitsyn was hoisted into the Soviet literary establishment. For three years he enjoyed its perquisites to the full. Meanwhile a time bomb was ticking: the material on which he was working or was about to publish could scarcely fail to explode his new found security. Warnings were not long in coming: in 1964 the fall of his "patron" Khrushchev and the consolidation of party rigidity in the guise of Leonid Brezhnev; in 1965, in the very same month of September, the arrest of Sinyavsky and Daniel, and a KGB raid on Solzhenitsyn's "archive," from which, along with several typed copies of *The First Circle,* the police carried off one of his most damaging early manuscripts.

Perhaps he should have known that his struggle was in vain. But he continued to fight on for nearly another decade in the hope of getting his work before the Russian people and in the process preserving a measure of freedom for Russian literature. By the time of the KGB raid, a shortened version of *The First Circle* was ready for publication. Although once again Tvardovsky had vetted and admired it, his nervousness about getting it past the censor had inaugurated a misunderstanding and eventual rupture between him and the author which betokened how intransigent Solzhenitsyn was becoming. Yet even as abridged, *The First Circle* took a large step beyond *Ivan Denisovich.* Much longer, it was equally compact (only four days) and even more meticulously crafted. And now the cast of characters extended beyond the prisoners in the sharashka to the higher reaches of Soviet society and through them to Stalin in person, grimly portrayed at night in the Kremlin, "growing old like a dog, . . . filled . . . with helpless terror." If even *he* was afraid, could anyone in his whole vast dominions feel safe? To underline the point, Solzhenitsyn exploited his own twenty-year-old memory of a totally unexpected fall from grace. He told of a "gilded youth," an ultraprivileged young diplomat, who in the sudden realization that he had "only one life . . . only one conscience," committed a "treasonous" act which eventually brought him to interrogation, stripped of his trappings of high status, but "with his head held high."[14]

Its publication sidetracked, *The First Circle* was soon circulating in samizdat. And in 1968, with the author's permission, it appeared in translation in the West. Possibly this year, decisive in so many apparently unrelated European contexts, rather than that of the KGB raid three years earlier, marked the irrevocable shift in Solzhenitsyn's center of gravity, a shift of which he himself only little by little became aware. For one thing he had found a new audience abroad to replace the one denied him at home. And these Western readers greeted his novel with a reassuring rapture. For another, if even *The First Circle,* which for all its outspokenness depicted only the outer rim of the inferno, had landed him in grave difficulties, what would happen if and when the authorities, sifting the fragments of evidence they had in their hands, finally knew that he was already writing the series of volumes that would tell the whole story of what his people had suffered and, on a reduced scale, were suffering still?

By the mid-1960s Solzhenitsyn, aided by literally hundreds of informants, researchers, and typists, was hard at work on the colossal project which eventually became the three thick volumes of *The Gulag Archipelago.* He went at his task with somber, disciplined determination—with a sense of religious mission. "The . . . scope of this story and of this truth," he admitted, was "beyond the capabilities of one lonely pen." All he had "had was a peephole into the Archipelago." (But "to taste the sea all one needs is one gulp.") At the very least he could convey the dissolution of "the personality into feces and ash," the "feeling of universal innocence . . . the sense of an ordeal of the entire people," in which "the experience of the upper and the lower strata of society *merged*"—in short, the essence of what he had distilled from his own recollections and those of fellow ex-prisoners.[15]

A hybrid work without visible structure—a mélange of history and statistics, memoir and polemic, its tone oscillating between heavy irony and unbridled rage—*The Gulag Archipelago* did more than expose the full truth of what by now nearly all educated people, in the Soviet Union and in the West alike, had some inkling. It also began to open the eyes of Solzhenitsyn's readers to the extent of his ideological shift to the right. If *Ivan Denisovich* (by stretching a bit) could be interpreted as within the confines of Party loyalty, and *The First Circle* had been embraced enthusiastically by Western-style democrats, *The Gulag Archipelago* left no grounds for such wishful thinking on the part of those whose respect for its author remained unbounded. Solzhenitsyn's nostalgia for Russia's past could no longer be explained away or denied —witness the almost affectionate tone in which he depicted (quite correctly) traditional serfdom as "merciful" when contrasted with the hell of life in the camps.[16]

The publication of the first volume in Paris at the end of 1973 sealed Solzhenitsyn's fate. (We have already noted the jolt it gave to French intellectuals of the Left.) Seven weeks later he was bundled into a plane bound for West Germany, there to be welcomed by Heinrich Böll, like himself a Nobel laureate and the only major Western writer he knew well enough to call a friend. From Böll's home he went on to Switzerland and eventually to the United States. By 1976 he had ensconced himself in rural Vermont, in a house surrounded by fifty acres of land, which he further surrounded by a chain-link fence. Here, in a countryside sufficiently reminiscent of Russia to assure his peace of mind, he settled into the life of a recluse, receiving only chosen visitors and, aside from increasingly infrequent forays into public polemic, devoting himself solely to his writing in the rigorously disciplined fashion that by now had become second nature.

The work with which Solzhenitsyn occupied his exile far surpassed in scale anything he had produced before; by that fact alone it seemed to rule out full translation into English. An epic of more than Tolstoyan dimensions, it harked back to his earliest ambition: to tell the story of his country's transformation by the First World War and the revolutions of 1917. But where once he had intended to compose a celebration of Leninist values, by the time he actually started writing, the work had become the very opposite: the record of a slide into catastrophe. Two slim volumes gave a foretaste of what was to come. *August 1914,* in which the author's father figured, narrated the Russian defeat on the same "metaphysical" terrain (to borrow Tournier's expression) on which he himself had suffered disgrace three decades later. *Lenin in Zürich* reflected his own stay in Switzerland at the start of his exile. The account of another exile's impatient waiting for the signal to go home and lead a revolution, it disconcerted readers by a lingering ambivalence, as Solzhenitsyn added up his final reckoning with his original ideological hero. These two books, however, were mere fragments.[17] When the full scope of the epic began to unfold, the overall design emerged: it was to consist of a series of historic "knots" or "nodal points," each named after and concentrated on an individual month. Part fact and part fiction, the successive volumes were packed with exhaustive detail. By the late 1980s the end was not yet in sight.

By that time, those who could read Solzhenitsyn in Russian consisted primarily of émigrés like himself. Indeed, to extend a hand to them ranked as one of his major aims: to bring them back into the Russian fold, "to restore unity to his divided and suffering people." This ambition stood at the emotional center of his endeavors. With his tone sounding ever more prophetic (or possibly messianic), he eventually came to view himself as the "sole spokesman" qualified to reinterpret the history of his unhappy countrymen and thereby to voice their longings.[18] Hence his growing egoism as well as his growing harshness toward his first wife, toward his editor, Tvardovsky, toward so many who had loved and aided him in his ascent to greatness. From his lonely eminence he now hurled verbal thunderbolts with an even-handed conviction of righteousness. Nor did he spare the hosts who had given him shelter: the West stood accused of loss of "civil courage" and of "spiritual exhaustion."[19]

"Our only living classic"—so one of his fellow writers had hailed him. In the literary judgment his readers could concur. But they did not necessarily agree with Solzhenitsyn's polemical stance. Far from it. As the reactionary, authoritarian, and even theocratic character of this stance became transparently evident, so its atypical quality in the spectrum of Soviet dissent became equally apparent. Solzhenitsyn had always kept his distance from the main body of dissidents. As the years went on, his marginality increased. After a promising start, his relations with the greatest of them, Andrei Sakharov, veered off into antagonism. And for good reason. Where Solzhenitsyn reincarnated the aspirations of the nineteenth-century Slavophiles, Sakharov did the same for contemporary Westernizers. And the words of the latter found a wider response both in Russia and abroad.

These "Westernizers"—intellectuals for the most part, and frequently the children of people who had suffered or perished under Stalin's tyranny—at first were known as the democratic movement and subsequently as the movement for human rights (although the two terms remained interchangeable). But to call them a movement is to fall into misplaced concreteness. Seldom numbering more than a thousand active participants, with a steady turnover in "membership" as repression thinned their ranks, they lacked formal structure or regulations.[20] Rather, they constituted a loose, far-flung (though Moscow-based) network, tied one to another by friendship and mutual trust and scarcely needing to define their goals, because these appeared self-evident.

The human rights movement may be dated either from December 1965, when forty or more people, mainly students, gathered in Pushkin Square to protest the jailing of Sinyavsky and Daniel and to demand respect for the Soviet constitution, or from the year of decision elsewhere (and in Solzhenitsyn's life), 1968. In that year Sakharov fired his first shot; in that year the most tenacious and influential of samizdat journals published its first issue.

Before assessing these, it may be well to review the human rights movement's successive incarnations. Two salient features emerge from such a review: a strict adherence to legality; and a cumulative effort to reach out for support to well-wishers abroad.

The legalist emphasis may remind us of KOR's principle of behaving "as if" Poland were a free society. Similarly in the Soviet Union, human-rights workers acted the part of free men and women. "On their own initiative" they "exercised the civil rights guaranteed by the Soviet constitution: freedom of speech and of the press, the right to public demonstration and to free association." They also learned how to exploit legal loopholes. If, for example, they constituted themselves "as an association of authors, . . . neither permission from the authorities nor even official registration" was required.[21]

Such was true of their second incarnation, the Committee for Human Rights, which in late 1970 developed from the first, an Initiative Group gathered together the previous year. Hovering in a status of quasi-legality, the new committee took the unprecedented step of affiliating with an international body, the League of Human Rights. Previously only officially endorsed Soviet associations had been able to do so. With this precedent established, the human rights movement went on to forge two additional international links: in 1974 its core metamorphosed into the Soviet chapter of Amnesty International; in 1976 it established the Moscow Helsinki Watch Group. Yet even in this fourth incarnation, its boldest to date, it remained within the bounds of legality. For the Final Act of the Helsinki accords, signed the previous year by the Soviet government, had appealed to the citizens of the signatory nations to help in monitoring the observance of the human rights specified in that document.[22]

Although the Helsinki accords of 1975 marked the high point of détente between the United States and the Soviet Union, they did little to relieve official pressure on Soviet dissent. Throughout the period of détente the KGB maintained its familiar routines. Whether a diminution of vigilance took place following a crackdown in the early 1970s has been much debated. Something must have changed to permit such efforts as Amnesty International and Helsinki Watch to become "a visible presence in Moscow," and "Brezhnev's relaxed attitude toward official corruption complemented" an "equivocal policy on dissent."[23] But by the end of the decade, with the Soviet leader's health failing, the KGB could gird itself for a second assault. And on Brezhnev's death in 1982, the accession of the man who headed that body, Yuri Andropov, spelled doom for dissidents. By early 1984, when in turn Andropov succumbed, his former associates had accomplished their objective: by that "Orwellian" year, they had broken the back of the organized opposition through imprisonment, forced exile, and the novel, subtly excruciating technique of confinement in psychiatric wards.

That all was not lost, that a handful of brave souls continued to protest, was apparent in the vicissitudes of the *Chronicle of Current Events* and in the lonely ordeal of Andrei Sakharov.

Nothing remotely resembling the *Chronicle* had appeared in the Soviet Union since the 1920s. "Although modest in scope and appearance," it "contained real news, uncensored news, gathered by a staff of sorts that had talked with unfettered sources of information and that, in some cases, had directly witnessed events and freely written about them . . . What the *Chronicle* reported one would not find in *Pravda, Izvestia,"* and the other "state-monitored mass media." Its "editors," a shifting, amorphous group, with the constant turnover that arrests entailed, strove for factual accuracy and an unemotional tone. They also tried to remain scrupulously legal, an impossible feat, since they found themselves driven against their will to the techniques of clandestine publication. After betrayal within their ranks had imposed on them a silence of eighteen months, their reliance on underground methods became even more pronounced. They worked in "concentric circles," with only those at the very center doing the final assembling and editing. The ordinary reader who wanted to pass information was given a stern admonition: "Simply tell it to the person from whom you received the *Chronicle,* and he will tell the person from whom *he* received the *Chronicle,* and so on. But do not try to trace back the whole chain of communication yourself, or else you will be taken for a police informer." How many people read the *Chronicle?* Estimates ran all the way from ten thousand to one hundred thousand. But even if we accept the lower figure, we must recognize that this readership was drawn from the authentic elite of Soviet society. Above all we must recall that the *Chronicle,* which survived no less than five KGB campaigns against it, was a unique beacon of honesty in a land of officially sponsored lies.[24]

Meantime, Andrei Sakharov had step by step evolved toward a position correspondingly central and correspondingly symbolic. Three years younger than Solzhenitsyn, he came from more exalted origins and with a youthful experience nowhere near so troubled. Quite the contrary; by Russian standards he could be considered pampered. The son of a physicist and himself the boy wonder of Soviet physics, he was exempted from military service during the Second

World War and eventually assigned to the comfortable, privileged isolation of a science city. Here he "fathered" the Soviet hydrogen bomb. Here his mounting doubts about his
own achievement led him by the late 1950s to advocate the
suspension of nuclear testing. By the mid-1960s he was
joining more than twenty other leading intellectuals in an
open warning against neo-Stalinism. Subsequently he helped
found the Committee for Human Rights. In the fateful year
1968, not without inner torment, he crossed the boundary
between the Soviet establishment and Soviet dissent: he published in samizdat and abroad his first book, *Reflections* [or
Thoughts] *on Progress, Peaceful Coexistence, and Intellectual
Freedom*.

From this point there was no turning back. Sakharov had
become a dissident, and the leading figure among the Westernizers. And, despite constant and growing harassment by
the police and the official press, he determined to stick it out
at home. He would not emigrate or even travel—more particularly since, with the expulsion of Solzhenitsyn, he had
become irreplaceable. (For all their disagreements, Sakharov
continued to admire Solzhenitsyn as "a giant in the struggle
for human dignity.") At length, at a loss to know what to do
with Sakharov, and, in view of his fame abroad, evidently
loath to send him to a penal camp, the government exiled him
to the provincial city of Gorky. There he remained for six
long years, hounded, humiliated, cut off from nearly all
outside contact, and twice endangering his weak heart with a
hunger strike and the painful ordeal of forced feeding that
followed.[25] In December 1986 his fortitude at long last received its reward: the new master of the Russians, Mikhail
Gorbachev, invited him back to Moscow, there to resume his
scientific labors and, on a reduced scale, his public defense of
human rights.

Sakharov's first book had been infused with an optimism
that had soon waned. By his own admission, the "general
tenor" of *Progress, Coexistence, and Intellectual Freedom* re-

flected "the time of its writing—the height of the 'Prague Spring.'" In it he had proclaimed his faith in the eventual "convergence" of the Soviet and the Western systems of government and society, in an "inevitable process of rapproachement": the one would become freer, the other more socialist. He had even gone so far as to propose that democratization could be "carried out under the direction" of his own country's Communist Party.[26]

In subsequent writings Sakharov's tone shifted to one of warning and a growing reliance on the West.[27] Not only did he voice a newly discovered skepticism about socialist theory and practice. He underlined the danger of détente or rapproachement without an accompanying program of democratization in the Soviet Union. He called on the United States to lead in a unified Western strategy. But along with this sharpened set of recommendations went a continued insistence on humane values. Sakharov never allowed himself to be transmuted into a "cold warrior." He stood unflinchingly for the "absolute priority" of arms negotiations, and he resisted the notion of "the destruction or total condemnation" of abhorrent regimes. In short—and here lay his great strength and distinctiveness—he viewed matters from a global standpoint, championing the right of human beings to move about and to live in freedom wherever they might choose. As a citizen of the world he incarnated what was widest in range in the varied spectrum of Soviet dissent.

By the time of Sakharov's return to Moscow, Soviet dissent, for all its heroism and sacrifice, had been reduced to a tiny cohort. One estimate suggested that its activist component, those willing to "take public roles," was down to no more than thirty people, reinforced, it was true, by many, many more in an "invisible region," from which a volunteer could periodically be drawn to replace someone arrested.[28] Beyond this region, uncertain and fluctuating in extent, the dissidents had failed to penetrate the spongy mass of the vast apathetic majority. Bureaucrats and managers equated freedom with disorder and preferred to bear the ills they had than to plunge into the painful process of fundamental reform. As for the class from which the bulk of the dissidents came—the intelligentsia of writers and artists—these too for the most part refrained from taking a stand. In privacy or in the security of a noisy, tipsy, uninhibited social gathering, they might readily agree to dismiss the regime as barbarous. But they would not risk being stripped of their privileges: the special shops, high-standard medical care, preferential housing, dachas, and resorts to which their status entitled them. And, still more insidiously, they rationalized their prudence by finding dissent naive or possibly counterproductive, and its exponents self-righteous men and women, their egos inflated by a traditional and familiar Russian "martyr-complex."[29]

"Now, albeit with caution, everybody curses the authorities, makes sarcastic remarks in lines and in street cars, and doormen and members of the Central Committee crack political jokes." Thus one Soviet citizen, alert to shifts in public temper, defined the change that the new phenomenon of political opposition had brought about. Or, in the words of an American student of the subject: "The dissidents did not think differently from everyone else, as the word *dissent* implies. Rather, they decided to say" what was already common knowledge.[30] At least such was true of the elite that counted. Looked at from this perspective—the perspective of the disabused, sophisticated observer, unwilling to take a chance but possibly with grudging respect for those who did—Soviet dissent had made a difference after all.

It had made a difference even in legal procedures. As the protracted police pursuit of the *Chronicle of Current Events* proved—a pursuit in which a mountain of documents and hundreds of agents figured—the growing insistence on basic civil rights had persuaded the authorities that at least "a pretense of rule of law" was now required. Even the KGB found "itself bound by unwritten Soviet convention" to that effect; whatever brutalities might be committed along the way, the leadership had excluded any full-blown return to Stalinist terror.[31]

Finally, among its other unheralded accomplishments, Soviet dissent had inaugurated the process which Solzhenitsyn held so dear, reknitting the world of Russian culture within the Soviet Union to the one beyond its borders. By the late 1980s the "third wave" of emigration to the West had become a flood: something like half of Russia's leading creative figures now lived in France, in Germany, and in the United States. As opposed to the first wave (refugees from the Revolution or the Civil War) or the second (the displaced persons of 1945), these new émigrés succeeded in maintaining ties to their homeland. Despite intense internecine bickering, they were bound together by nostalgia and by "hopeful communication with those they left behind."[32] They sent and received letters, they made international telephone calls, they read in editions published in Paris or West Germany the same works that circulated within the Soviet Union in samizdat or, more miraculously continued to appear "above ground."

This last was true of a novelist whom all varieties of Russians could read and who wrote of and for the educated but apolitical, the realists who managed to survive and even prosper. Like the great editor Tvardovsky (who published his work), Yuri Trifonov had learned to test the limits of the permissible, to make his point within the interstices of the system. For this and for his success with the wider public, Trifonov stood accused of cynicism. Nothing could be farther from the truth: his later work was suffused with deep moral feeling and by a faith in "absolute values." The determining feature of his adolescence was that he "grew up half in and half out of the élite," somewhere between Solzhenitsyn's precarious status and Sakharov's privileged youth. The son of a Red Army commander, at the age of twelve Trifonov had suffered the searing experience of his father's disappearance in the great purge of the 1930s, soon to be followed by that of his mother. The inevitable Russian grandmother had carried on with his upbringing, and he had gotten off to a quick start as a novelist writing in the accepted style and receiving a Stalin Prize in his mid-twenties. Thereafter, as though he had begun to recognize the hollowness of this sort of success, over a long period of self-doubt he changed course. "He spent the years of the Thaw under Khrushchev, when so many other young talents were blossoming, in the state archives seeking to rehabilitate his father's memory, and he achieved his own artistic liberation in the decade when other writers were being expelled or silenced."[33]

The "new Trifonov" who emerged in the mid-1960s had only sixteen more years to live. But in that decade and a half he produced what ranked as the very best in officially permitted Russian literature. In a succession of short novels, dense with ambiguously conveyed meanings, rich with psychological perception, and culminating in *The Old Man,* which was published in 1978, three years before his death, he exposed gently and indulgently the pettiness he saw about him. He wrote about intrigues for better living quarters, for perquisites, for promotions; he wrote of people like himself, Muscovites for the most part, in a fashion that both shocked and enthralled. For with an exquisite attention to telling detail, he conveyed to his readers what they already knew about themselves but had not yet found in print. (In this respect, although he remained aloof from the dissidents, he did a job comparable to theirs.)

Much of what he related, although crafty and self-seeking, was relatively harmless. But in his finest novel, *The House on the Embankment,* he rose to the sterner stuff of betrayal—the half-conscious betrayal of an elderly professor by a favorite student, and his daughter's fiancé. Into the career of this far from admirable protagonist, Trifonov inserted elements from his own past—just as in *The Old Man* he told of an obstinate quest to document the unjust execution of a Cossack general of the Civil War.[34] "Look," Trifonov seemed to be admonishing his readers, "this is what we are," pygmies when compared to the heroic generation of the fathers, who had fought and died for Bolshevik values, however mistaken these had subsequently proved.

That loyalty to Bolshevik values flickered on in the gray, depressing Russia of Leonid Brezhnev was evidenced by the career of another insider-outsider, Roy Medvedev, who resembled Trifonov in inspiring distrust among strict dissidents. He too in the purge of the late 1930s had lost his father, in this case a professor of history at a military academy. In spite of this, the young man had chosen to pursue his father's profession (unlike his twin brother, Zhores, who became a biologist), although he never reached the academic heights. Perhaps early on he showed an independence of mind that blocked his promotion; not until Khrushchev had spoken out against the crimes of Stalin did he become a party member. And those crimes were to offer the grand theme for his own writings, notably in *Let History Judge,* which, after its author had vainly attempted official publication, began to circulate in samizdat and appeared in 1971 in the West. Meantime his brother had been stripped of his passport (in effect exiled) while traveling abroad, and he himself had been similarly deprived of party membership and dismissed from his modest professional job.[35] Nothing daunted, Roy Medvedev carried on as a private scholar, absorbed in historical research, occasionally interviewed by a foreign journalist, watched closely by the KGB, but otherwise unmolested.

He had earlier worked closely with Sakharov—as Sakharov had earlier found ground for understanding with Solzhenitsyn. But as the attitudes of the trio eventually sorted themselves out, they ended up in three distinct positions, with Solzhenitsyn to the right, Sakharov in the center, and Medvedev on the left. This last position long figured as the most quixotic. Speaking for those who called themselves a loyal opposition, or "party-democrats," Medvedev advocated democratization of Soviet government and society within the system itself by "restoring" and "developing Leninist norms." Quite aside from the dubiousness of Lenin's respect for democracy, the party-democratic position rested on shaky foundations. By Medvedev's own admission, it was "the weakest trend" among the three. It enjoyed virtually no support at the top of the Soviet hierarchy and could do no better than to *claim* support among young party members and the intelligentsia. Moreover, on the key question of political organizations in competition with the Communist, it sounded defeatist: "A new opposition party, even if sanctioned by the authorities, could not count on any significant . . . success." Yet far from succumbing to discouragement, Medvedev ended his basic work, *On Socialist Democracy,* with a utopian forecast: "By the end of the twentieth century there will no longer be peasants or workers or office workers or intelligentsia in the original sense of those terms. The population of our country will consist largely of well-educated, cultured human beings."[36]

These words saw the light in 1972. During the bleak twelve years that followed, despite mounting evidence to the contrary, Medvedev stuck to his advocacy of democratization from within. Unremitting in his insistence on nonviolence and tolerance toward those with whom one disagreed, he scanned the horizon for signs that party-democracy had not expired. Abroad he found it in Eurocommunism. At home he found it in "an honest engineer, scientist, factory manager, director of a scientific institute, . . . official in the party apparatus, or . . . military officer" who was doing "good for the progressive and democratic development" of Soviet society while remaining "within the system." The old style of dissent, he maintained, was "dying"; a "chapter" had ended. Now "a new generation" was "working . . . to pick up the ball," a generation whose methods bespoke "greater profundity."[37] Presumably

Medvedev meant realism of the cautious step-by-step variety. Once more we find in his analysis the same odd mixture of modest means and soaring hopes.

In the early months of 1987 Roy Medvedev emerged from the shadows; suddenly his name and his views began to appear in the Western press. The sight of the newly rehabilitated Sakharov applauding a speech by Gorbachev, the release of more than one hundred and fifty additional prominent dissidents, the beginnings of another thaw in literature and the arts, an official assault on the legacy of Stalin more thoroughgoing than even Khrushchev had mounted— all these taken together gave grounds for hope. Along with them the vision of a lonely and idiosyncratic man, while not precisely vindicated, took on new relevance for the still uncharted future of Soviet society.

EIGHT

Democratic Socialism: North and South

Peering out toward the West from his beleaguerment in Moscow, Roy Medvedev glimpsed evidence of an encouraging change in democratic socialism. Not only had it widened its geographical range, with "the liquidation of the last of the fascist regimes, in Portugal, Spain, and Greece"; it was manifesting a new concern for "the quality of life" and was attenuating its ingrained hostility toward Communism. (For his part Medvedev recognized the "limitations" of his own comparably ingrained respect for Lenin, for what he was now prepared to call *"yesterday's Marxism."*) In Italy he welcomed Communism "with a new political face"; elsewhere he discovered Socialists pursuing "more radical, more decisive policies." The union of these two forces, he argued, offered the greatest hope for social progress in Western Europe and for "the development of democratic tendencies in the Eastern bloc."[1]

To what extent did this prospectus correspond to reality, whether political or in the realm of ideas? For intellectuals it came too late. By the early 1980s, when Medvedev launched his appeal to the West, the majority, even of the left-inclined, had given up on Marxism. In Soviet behavior, they could discern scarcely a trace of the ideology still proclaimed. The ossified regime Brezhnev controlled had long since lost its capacity either to attract or to inspire any deep-seated fear;

for once, judgments on the right and judgments on the left were in accord. As for the "Western" Marxism deriving from Antonio Gramsci and the Frankfurt School, after a period of intense cultivation in the 1960s and early 1970s, it too had gone into decline.

Its disappointments had proved too many—the last and greatest being "the collapse of Eurocommunism," when the French pulled out, leaving the Italians to carry on alone.[2] If the Italian Communist party stood isolated among its Western counterparts in championing democratic values and procedures, it was also the only one that made an impressive showing at the polls. On the level of practical politics, then, Medvedev's notion of a union among the forces of the Left had been overtaken by events. Of the prospective partners, the Communists counted in one country alone, and there they could best be reckoned as belonging in the essentials to the democratic socialist camp.

However mistaken Medvedev might be in overestimating Communism's Western potential, he was on target in detecting signs of renewal in the theory and practice of what northern parties called Labor or Social Democracy and southern simply Socialism. An ideology that for decades had appeared moribund had begun to show signs of life. No longer did intellectuals of the far Left wield a near-monopoly on critical speculation. Democratic socialists of moderate persuasion, only tangentially if at all indebted to Marx, were starting to rethink and to solidify their basic tenets. Along with them a succession of genuinely charismatic leaders were evoking an equally genuine popular response. A crucial doubt, however, remained: could democratic socialism achieve the apparently incompatible goals of, on the one hand, stopping conservative resurgence in its tracks and, on the other, striking out on its own with sufficient boldness to head off competition from new movements oriented toward issues just now coming into view?

On the intellectual front, a plethora of contestants dictates a selective treatment. One theoretician, Jürgen Habermas, and one international gathering, the 1985 conference held under Yugoslav auspices at Cavtat on the Adriatic, may stand for the rest.

Habermas was at once exemplary and atypical. A belated *Freischwebender,* awesome in the variety of his interests, he epitomized what democratic socialism needed most: honesty, good sense, a strong critical thrust, and an aversion to the doctrinaire. In the era of student effervescence he had warned the young against the self-defeating nature of their movement. Nearly a decade later, in 1977, he sounded a corresponding warning against the overreaction on the German Right to a wave of terrorism.[3] Serenely, even-handedly, he stuck to the course he had charted as early as 1968 (that same year!) with his first major study, *Knowledge and Human Interests.* In his own words, he aimed to combine knowledge and interest in an approach which would be alike "cognitive" and "emancipatory." In the words of his authoritative expositor, he little by little composed a theory that was empirical without laying claim to strict scientific status; "historical without being historicist; and . . . practical, not in the sense of possessing a technological potential but in the sense of being oriented" toward social change.[4]

Born in 1929 to middle-class parents in a small south German town, Habermas grew up in a conventional milieu where Nazism (which attained power as he was turning four) seems to have been taken for granted. He served in the Hitler Youth and at the age of fifteen "was sent to man the western defenses" by a regime reduced to desperate expedients. Suddenly his "own history was . . . cast in a light that made all its essential aspects appear radically different. All at once" he saw that he "had been living in a politically criminal system."[5] Such was the first of two great awakenings in his ideological and intellectual life.

120

The second came after a decade of preparation. Habermas found his original university studies, at Göttingen and Bonn, disappointing. With the German academic community, despite its liberation from tyranny, not yet "opened up to outside influences," the professors were continuing to teach "in a provincial German context." Left to his own devices, he discovered Marx and Sartre, as much later he was to work his way through Wittgenstein and through American pragmatism and sociology. By his mid-twenties his philosophical and his political interests, which up to then had been proceeding along separate tracks, were beginning "to come together."[6]

In 1956 the decisive convergence occurred. Two events launched Habermas on his way. Now in Frankfurt, he heard the Freud centennial lectures, in which "the international elite" reintroduced psychoanalytic theory to the German intellectual world; he also became assistant to Theodor W. Adorno, back from his American exile and at the height of his influence. To Habermas, Adorno threw open the gates to the richly endowed and multifaceted realm of what subsequently became known as the Frankfurt School. A reading of its boldest work, *Dialectic of Enlightenment,* the younger man recalled as a "revelation." In the public mind he ranked as the school's most gifted heir. He himself insisted on his divergence from philosophical masters to whom he readily acknowledged a profound indebtedness. Besides the biographical difference of being a generation younger than they—with non-Jewish parents who had never emigrated— he shared neither their antiempirical bent nor their fidelity to a Hegelian "concept of truth," which he found "irreconcilable with the fallibility of scientific endeavor." Moreover, Habermas was less pessimistic and more oriented toward politics. These temperamental preferences drew him to that deviant former member of the Frankfurt School, Herbert Marcuse, for whom he "felt a special affinity," whose *Eros and*

Civilization touched him with "its direct political resonance," and over whose last hours he was to watch with tender solicitude.[7]

Yet even Marcuse, along with Adorno and the rest, incurred the reproach of never having taken "bourgeois democracy very seriously." For Habermas that democracy, for all its failings, figured as a basic given—at the very least a point of departure for deep structural reform. Although he valued "being considered a Marxist," he preferred "a political culture, which, like the American," sprang from the eighteenth-century Enlightenment. He spoke English with ease and visited the United States again and again, where he marveled "at the intellectual openness and readiness for discussion" of the American students he encountered. His "unbelievable compulsion to synthesize" might puzzle his friends across the Atlantic, but they found him a congenial companion.[8]

Delicately poised on the boundary between left liberalism and Western Marxism, in his own country Habermas voted for the Social Democrats. He did so without illusion—through recognizing that there was no turning back from contemporary industrial society (as Adorno and Marcuse had sometimes seemed to imagine), that capitalism had shown and was still showing an unexpected resilience, and that in these circumstances what he called "the welfare-state compromise" had to be both endorsed and buttressed. In a strict economic sense Habermas defined socialism in minimalist fashion. What concerned him above all, as in his writings he turned increasingly from abstraction to the "life-world," was "the pressure of suffering" on "the margins of society." It was to these, he maintained, that class conflict, which in its classic form was languishing "in a state of suspension," had shifted its axis. "Human dignity" had become the centerpiece of a modest, down-to-earth notion of a better society. "Every individual," Habermas concluded, "should be unmolested in his or her autonomy, protected in his or her physical and spiritual integrity." Yet "the individual cannot be free unless all are free, and all cannot be free unless all are free in community."[9]

Implicit in Habermas' theoretical writings and public polemics was a constant self-questioning about socialism's future in an economic and class setting that bore scant resemblance to the context in which that ideology had been conceived. Such also was the agenda the Cavtat conference set itself: to assess the prospects for democratic socialist faith and practice "on the threshhold of the twenty-first century."

Amid a welter of pious hopes and repetition, three dominant themes emerged. The first was a counsel of caution, voiced by a Frenchwoman, Colette Audry. "The road to socialism," she reminded the gathering, had proved more protracted, "less direct and infinitely more difficult" than had originally been imagined. No longer could one hold to the conviction which had sustained previous generations of militants that socialism represented "a *guaranteed future* for mankind."[10] If such was the case—and nobody seemed inclined to dispute it—how could one preserve and redeploy socialism as a viable ideology for the new century which was already in sight? The answer came in the second and third themes, themes that were in only apparent contradiction: socialist thinking needed to enlarge its scope in order to reckon with a world economy that was producing unfamiliar patterns of exploitation; such thinking needed to fall back on its "elementary humane core."

Pietro Ingrao, a thoughtful and respected Italian Communist leader, spelled out the implications of a world economy "reaching completion." Besides pinpointing the menace of ecological degradation and nuclear catastrophe, he traced the path by which "the great multinational oligopolies" had brought about an unprecedented and intractable type of social stratification. On the one hand, they had centralized "the planning operations carried out by the 'brains' of the enterprise"; on the other hand, they had decentralized "the various stages of production to different parts of the world." The result was a mounting disparity in the situation of the laboring classes—between that of skilled workers at the center, who enjoyed relative security, and "the widespread mass of insecure casual workers, unemployed or jobless youngsters, and women," drifting "precariously in and out of the labor market." Moreover, with the diffusion of education and the development of "powerful means of mass information," the gap was growing "ever wider between the skills actually possessed by individuals" and the "deskilled" work they performed, "between the creative potential of human beings and the uses to which that potential" was put.[11] The most pressing task for a socialism oriented toward the future, Ingrao implied, was to devise ways to close the gap.

It was left for a Scandinavian, Göran Therborn, to remind the gathering that socialists could not even begin to do so unless they consolidated their base in the Western world. On the most elementary level such a consolidation meant defense of the welfare state. With slums and poverty becoming "more and more widespread in British and American cities, the dangers involved in a roll-back of the welfare state should be obvious to any humane person." On a more exalted plane, consolidation meant rehabilitating the word "injustice," which, although cherished by old-line democratic socialists like Jean Jaurès, had never figured in "the Standard Marxist dictionary." Above and beyond that, the restoration of time-honored verities meant renewing the socialist vision of "giving every man and woman upon this earth the economic, social and political possibility of a pursuit of happiness." "No more" than that, Therborn concluded, with a disarming show of modesty, but certainly "no less." In short, socialism should be redefined as a "project for a universal humanism."[12]

124

In the realm of practice, another Scandinavian, the Swedish prime minister Olof Palme, picked up a leitmotif already sounded by the intellectuals of the democratic Left, a theme that, strictly speaking, was not socialist at all. On a night of electoral triumph in September 1985 he wearily, almost shyly, voiced his deeply felt conviction: "With all its faults, the welfare state" remained "the most humane and civilized system ever created." Five months later he perished at the hands of an assassin.

Although Palme was gone, the variety of Socialist leadership he epitomized lived on: flexible, outgoing, good-humored, even charming, of a sort that people had learned not to expect from parties known, at least in their northern strongholds, for stodginess and bureaucratization. Palme's example and that of his West German counterpart, Willy Brandt, belied the stereotype of a sober, disciplined north as against a volatile, emotional south. Moreover, by the mid-1980s Socialists nearly everywhere, in their day-to-day management of affairs, if not always in their public pronouncements, were no longer concerned with "dismantling capitalism." Rather they subscribed to a "restrained Keynesianism" and to a set of goals or principles which an authoritative but unsympathetic British journal summarized as "economic justice, a fair distribution of wealth, equality of social opportunity."[13]

If Palme was the most colorful of the new brand of northern leaders, Brandt was the most influential and the most durable. As foreign minister in 1966 he had launched the program of reaching out toward the Soviet Union and the Communist-dominated rump of his severed country that became known as *Ostpolitik*. As chancellor from 1969 to 1974, his unconventionality and outspokenness attracted to his party disaffected writers and students who had no use for the customary routines of German politics. After leaving the chancellorship, he turned his energies outward. From 1976 on, as president of the Socialist International, he began to look south. He taught his fellow Socialists to take seriously the agonizing needs of the Third World, whose representatives he welcomed into the leadership of the International. He served as midwife for the reemergence of democracy— and eventually for Socialist rule—in the nations of southern Europe newly liberated from right-wing tyranny.

In Greece this had happened in 1974 with the collapse of army rule. In Spain it had come about in 1975 with the death of Francisco Franco. In both cases, after a transition phase of government by conservatives or centrists, Socialist parties had won decisive electoral victories under the guidance of forceful figures possessing a rare combination of immense popular radiance and tactical finesse. Andreas Papandreou, who became prime minister of Greece in 1981, and Felipe Gonzalez, who attained power in Spain a year later, shared a disregard for anticapitalist consistency and a cool pragmatism that seemed as "un-Mediterranean" as Palme or Brandt's impulsiveness looked "un-northern."

The same was true of Socialism in Italy, the central and key Mediterranean country. Patiently, tenaciously, and with a ruthless contempt for his rivals, Bettino Craxi had galvanized his somnolent party. He had simultaneously challenged the twin colossi of Italian politics, the Communists and the Christian Democrats, forcing the first to reckon with Socialist competition and the second to accede to his demand for the premiership, which, as the perennially strongest party, they had regarded as their own preserve. Craxi remained Italy's prime minister for an unprecedented three and a half years until his characteristically abrupt resignation in March 1987.

Leaders such as these originally looked to Brandt as a model. Closer to home, however, and more compelling, was a precedent from France—a precedent that, to the surprise and bitterness of one and all, proved "the example not to follow . . . the catalog of errors to avoid."[14]

Nineteen eighty-one was democratic socialism's year of triumph and decision. In May that year, by the narrowest of margins, François Mitterrand was elected president of France, carrying along with him a month later a majority of Socialists into the National Assembly. That December the Italian Communists completed a process of democratization which had been in the making for more than a decade.

Mitterrand's victory constituted a unique opportunity. Never before had the Socialist party of a major continental country received an unqualified mandate—and with it the chance (which had been hanging fire for a century) to enact a coherent program unimpeded by lukewarm allies. The new president was brimming over with confidence; so were his followers in the Assembly, nearly half of whom were schoolteachers. Their advent seemed to betoken a shift in the personal axis of French politics, away from the domination by an elite of technocrats that had lasted more than two decades, and toward greater human contact with the ordinary citizen and concern for the "humble." In his presidential campaign their leader had evoked reassuring images from a simpler past, notably a poster with a village steeple behind him, the two together radiating what he called *la force tranquille*. In his inaugural statement, with an old-fashioned humanist turn of phrase, Mitterrand summoned up the jovial memory of Jaurès, and to put through the reforms he had promised he appointed as premier not a ministerial veteran like himself, but a local worthy, the mayor of Lille, Pierre Mauroy, whose robust optimism incarnated the mentality of his party's rank and file.

In the first months of the new government reform legislation proceeded at a brisk clip: a thirty-nine-hour working week, longer paid vacations, higher social-security benefits, a lower retirement age—*and* massive nationalizations. Within a year it became apparent that the government was living beyond its means. In June 1982 it swung around to a policy of financial "rigor." In the same period of time, a single year, that it had taken Léon Blum's Popular Front to run up against an impassable *mur d'argent,* its heir, the better part of a half-century later, had ground to a halt.

One might be tempted to leave the matter there. But to do so would be to simplify beyond recognition the special circumstances that contributed to the failure of what now clearly ranked as the centerpiece of the democratic Left's revival. To begin with, Mitterrand—and more particularly his prime minister—placed undue stress on the nationalization of basic industrial and financial enterprise. Only this, they reckoned, could adequately mark their government as "socialist" rather than merely "social democratic," that is, a government that lived comfortably alongside large capital. For most of their ideological colleagues in neighboring countries, however, the distinction seemed little more than verbal, a distinction without content. For such as these, nationalization had ceased to figure among the essentials of the socialist faith. In short, to those beyond France's borders who were following with anxious sympathy what went on within, Mitterrand and Mauroy looked like stubborn fellows who had nailed their flag to an anachronism.

After local elections in 1983 proved that the French party's hold was slipping, the idiosyncratic character and background of its chief—which he had kept muted during a decade of ascent toward power—came to the foreground. With the erosion of his base, Mitterrand's own socialism began to erode. Or, more important, it began to emerge that he had never been a socialist at all. A veteran of the wartime Resistance, an implacable foe of De Gaulle's presidency and that of his two successors, he offered satisfactory credentials as a left democrat in a time-honored French tradition. But his assumption of command over France's Socialists had about it something of the contingent: they alone could provide the battalions his restless ambition required.

The military metaphor is apt. The new—or rather, old —Mitterrand who surfaced after the turning point of 1982–83, more and more often struck a nationalist, martial pose. He had always enjoyed disconcerting his innumerable friends (whom he treated with dignified reserve) by sudden changes of course; he had always been a gambler and an actor who relished the "mirrors game" of politics. But now his self-conscious stateliness took on contours of the "baroque." He surrounded himself in the Elysée Palace with what amounted to a court, a court which on occasion could include so deviant a writer as Michel Tournier. "Like a caged lion," Mitterrand strove to escape the straitjacket of economic rigor. One way he found to do so was to embark on multiple journeys abroad; he meddled in a succession of international crises; no more than De Gaulle could "he imagine for one moment that the history of the contemporary world" could "be resolved without him." And, most telling of all, on the Fourteenth of July 1983 he announced that he had changed his mind about France's independent nuclear deterrent; what he had once assailed he now embraced as his country's "sole means of defense."[15] In the presidential stance, in the presidential aura, those standing near him could detect a whiff of Bonapartism.

And so Mitterrand distanced himself from a party that no longer understood him[16]—or from a party that still understood him on one point alone. Early on, he had defined the ethic of the Left as "justice." And in the end, with one socialist position after another abandoned, this value remained as the heart of what he had intended to do. The definition of justice had in fact been narrowed: most of Mitterrand's hopes for integrating the Moslem immigrants from North Africa had fallen by the way. But one man at least had done all that could possibly have been expected of him: at the ministry of justice, Robert Badinter had restored the independence of the judiciary and the respect for personal dignity and civil rights which De Gaulle's conservative successors had grievously reduced.[17] Of all the accomplishments of the Mitterrand years, that of Badinter proved the most lasting.

In March 1986 the Socialists, not unexpectedly, lost their majority in the National Assembly. Along with them the Communists, with whom they had at first maintained an uneasy alliance, were punished far more by an electorate which seemed to judge them superfluous. Mitterrand stayed on as president—his term had two more years to run—regal in manner as ever and, paradoxically enough, enjoying greater public esteem than the victorious leaders of French conservatism with whom he was now obliged to "cohabit."

B y the turn of the decade Italy's Communists had virtually completed their protracted evolution toward democracy. Even in the depths of the Stalinist era their leader, Palmiro Togliatti, drawing on the teachings of his friend and master, Gramsci, had insisted on a plurality of communisms, as he struggled, for the most part sub rosa, to maintain a minimum of independence from Moscow. By 1964, with Stalin long dead and Khrushchev still in command, he was ready to summon up his courage for a final reckoning with a Kremlin he had served, however reluctantly, for nearly his whole political life. Just before his death at a sanatorium in the Crimea, he composed an ideological testament in which he explicitly endorsed "freedom of expression and debate, in the field of culture, art and in that of politics too."[18]

Togliatti's Yalta Memorandum liberated his party for the process of rethinking that culminated in 1981. Along the way the Italian Communists had supported Dubček against Brezhnev in 1968, had launched the promising, if ill-fated experiment of Eurocommunism, and had enjoyed an interlude on the margin of governmental responsibility in 1977–78. The last of these episodes marked the high point of their prestige and influence and bore the stamp of a new and younger leader, Enrico Berlinguer. A Sardinian nobleman by birth and an anti-Fascist by inheritance from his father, Berlinguer concealed under a shy and gracious manner an unbending determination to adapt Italian Communism to the realities of the late twentieth century. He went beyond discarding the Leninist goal of dictatorship of the proletariat; he went so far as to suggest that Gramsci's modification thereof as "hegemony" no longer sufficed.[19]

By December 1981, when General Jaruzelski proclaimed martial law in Poland, Berlinguer had brought his own troops into line for a concerted response. The collective leadership of the Italian Communist party voiced its "unequivocal condemnation of the military coup" which had "brutally disrupted" a process of "democratic renewal." For his own part, Berlinguer underlined the message by declaring that failure "to express an immediate and strong condemnation would have been an error of the first order." He added that other regimes besides the Polish, "based on the Soviet model," were currently "plunged in crisis." In these circumstances his own party's "defense of autonomy and free expression of views" had "in fact enlarged the scope" of its "internationalism"; the Italian Communists were "in a position to help communications between social democratic . . . movements on the one side and parties . . . whose beginnings related directly and indirectly to the October Revolution of 1917 on the other." In short, to borrow the phrase of a close colleague, the Italian Communists could "make a unique contribution" to the reunification of the European Left.[20]

It was not to be. Roy Medvedev's vision of an East-West ideological bridge glimmered on without substance. The untimely death of Enrico Berlinguer in 1984 deprived this vision of its most persuasive advocate, a loss from which Berlinguer's party had not yet recovered when it was called on to prove itself at the polls.

The Italian election of June 1987 was the last of a series of four which within the space of fifteen months dashed the hopes of the democratic Left. In every major western European country, socialism went down to defeat. We have seen how, in France, Mitterrand's party forfeited its majority in 1986. In January of the next year Germany's Social Democrats repeated—with a further drop in their vote—the reversal they had suffered in 1983. Five months later (and just three days before the election in Italy), the British Labour Party lost for the *third* successive time.

The Italian results were confused by the rivalry within the democratic Left between Communists and Socialists. While at 34.3 percent of the vote, the Christian Democrats maintained (and improved) their hegemonic position, Craxi's party jumped to 14.3 percent, and the Communists fell to 26.6—nearly eight percentage points below their electoral high-water mark of the mid 1970s. Here, as elsewhere, democratic socialism had shown itself unable to roll back the dominant conservative current. Nor had it mustered the imagination to rethink in a sufficiently radical fashion the basics of its political culture.

Defense of the welfare state had proved unavailing: the stalwarts of trade unionism who had sworn by it were a shrinking constituency, and the young seemed to find it boring or to take it for granted. Stress on justice was well and good—but possibly too abstract for electoral purposes. As for the nuclear issue, both the German and the British party had waffled, the former rather more so, the latter rather less.

At Cavtat the Italian Communist Ingrao had already sounded a warning. "Green movements," he had argued, "together with the peace movements," constituted "the most important new political (and intellectual) development of the . . . 1980s." He thought it a mistake to dismiss them "as epiphenomena" or "as mere romantic convolutions reacting to the tremendous developments of the 'machine age.'"[21] Ingrao's party tried to heed his advice. In the electoral campaign of 1987 it directed pointed appeals toward what it sensed as a new constituency. Again without avail. Greens,

132

now visible for the first time on the Italian political landscape, chalked up a crucial 2.5 percent of the vote, largely at Communist expense. In Germany five months earlier the results had been even more startling. The Greens had leapt from their 1983 score of 5.6 percent to 8.3; in comparative terms, of all the contestants they had gained the most. Europe's democratic socialists had failed to head off a new political culture which for the most part had caught them unaware.

NINE

The Triad of the Greens

On the death in 1985 of Heinrich Böll, the first German writer since Thomas Mann to receive the Nobel Prize, the Green leader Otto Schily paid tribute to his unique contribution to the rise of a new and youthful political culture. Böll, Schily noted, had defied the established institutions of the state and of industrial society and had even participated in a sit-in that was trying to block the installation of American nuclear missiles. In a "century of insincerity," he had told the truth "without conditions or limits." Yet he had done so with a gentleness, with a disarming irony, which reflected an open-minded Catholic upbringing in the Rhineland and a great "goodness of heart."[1] For the insurgent young he had ranked as a benevolent uncle, wise, indulgent, beloved—the conscience of the Federal Republic.

We have encountered Böll already in the role of Solzhenitsyn's first host after the Russian novelist's expulsion to the West. The two did not remain long together; if they had, their temperaments would certainly have clashed. All that bound them one to the other was a shared independence of spirit. Böll had none of Solzhenitsyn's fierce rage, his self-absorption, his overweening sense of an exalted mission; Böll spoke for more modest virtues. As an adolescent he had found the Nazis repellent, "on every level of . . . existence: conscious *and* instinctive, aesthetic *and* political."[2] It was said

134

that if one wanted to know what he thought, the safest bet was to propose precisely the opposite of what Hitler and his henchmen had believed and done. Böll stood for a good-humored and mutually supportive anarchy, for the absolute value of the unprotected individual, threatened on all sides. In attempting to resist the onslaughts of organized power (which Böll invariably depicted as evil), his protagonists never seemed quite sure of themselves, and they almost invariably suffered defeat.

In his early stories he had written about the Second World War service he had reluctantly performed and of the struggle to rebuild a life among his country's ruins. In his mature work he trained his sights on the hypocrisy and lingering authoritarianism he detected in postwar German democracy. Nor did he find these qualities in public institutions alone. He also took on the sensational daily press. In *The Lost Honor of Katharina Blum* (1974) he traced how step by step hounding by unscrupulous reporters had driven a decent, conscientious young woman to commit murder. (With lugubrious regularity, individuals of whose basic innocence Böll was convinced managed to land in prison!)

All these concerns came together in the ramifying *Group Portrait with Lady* (1971), which spanned four decades and three generations. Leaving its protagonist virtually a silent bystander, this novel spun the fine web of its plot by indirection, through successive testimonies as varied in style as they were in point of view. Its heterogeneous cast of characters included not only war widows, miscellaneous businessmen, and a "liberated" nun; it included, for the first time in major German fiction, a group of foreign workers, Portuguese as well as Turkish. And, what was more, it depicted them sympathetically.

Among the varied assortment of friends whom the protagonist, Leni, had gathered about her, the foreigners were "perhaps the most broad-minded."[3] Chiefly garbage-truck drivers and Leni's tenants (at rents below market value), they

135

organized the action that marked the climax of the novel—the carefully calculated collision of two of their monster vehicles—right at a crucial intersection, which tied up traffic for hours. Their purpose, ultimately successful, was to save their landlady from forced eviction. Through thus risking their own livelihoods, they raised their humble and despised profession to the level of heroism and an expression of human solidarity. Leni too, in her inarticulate fashion, had proved herself a heroine: in 1945—in this case at the risk of her life—she had born a son to a Russian prisoner of war. As the novel came to a close, she was about to bear another child to one of her Turkish tenants, who "on his knees and in a language unintelligible to her," had begged her for a favor she felt unable to refuse, because she could not endure seeing "anyone kneel to her."[4] Compassion—*Barmherzigkeit,* an eminently Catholic virtue—had for once triumphed in the end.

It should come as no surprise, then, that the author of such a novel should have supported the Greens in the Bundestag election of 1983. Had he lived, he would doubtless have done so again in 1987.

The dramatic rise in the Greens' vote from the first election to the second demonstrated that this new party (labeled "party" only because German law required it) was focusing on issues which the old, established political formations were neglecting, fudging, or dismissing with a few cursory phrases. These concerns had emerged at the future-oriented Cavtat conference. Yet the run of politicians of the democratic Left were proceeding in their familiar routines as though unaware of a potential constituency they were failing to reach. Greens challenged democratic socialists in particular to look at their society in a fresh perspective. They did this throughout Western Europe; but only in Germany did they become a force to be reckoned with.

The German Greens linked a triad of issues which together offered a new model for European political culture: ecology and the environment; rights of women; peace and the nuclear threat. At first glance these three might seem unrelated. Considered more closely, and with a small dose of rhetorical exaggeration, they could be viewed as having in common a protest against the disruption of the biological natural order by a male-dominated culture.[5]

When, in January 1980, the Greens formally constituted themselves a party, they had behind them a twelve-year buildup. In Germany the agitation among youth in general and students in particular which had erupted in 1968 had continued longer than elsewhere, leaving a heritage of diffused militancy. Veterans of 1968, grown more sober and sophisticated, along with a scattering of the middle-aged, chiefly the ecologically inclined, over the next decade had formed dozens of grassroots groups of activists. Most of the time they referred to themselves as "alternative," that is, proposing alternative courses to those pursued by the establishment. This view of the political and social world passed into the Green movement, as such groups little by little coalesced. The same was true of a "serious ethically-principled disposition," which distinguished them from a conventional party.[6]

What and how large was the constituency to which they could appeal? After the election of 1983 an American observer estimated their "passive support" as high "as 50–60 percent of the population." By this, however, he meant a generalized sympathy "on specific issues."[7] The Greens' electoral constituency could be reckoned at no more than a fifth of that figure. By the late 1980s they had not succeeded in becoming a mass movement. Although they championed the rights of marginal people and of foreign workers, they picked up few recruits among ordinary German members of the working classes. A profile of their deputies returned to the Bundestag in both 1983 and 1987 mirrored the constituency on which they drew: they were largely urban professionals, with an appeal primarily to the better educated and politically informed and to those aged eighteen to thirty-five. In the latter election they garnered 20 percent of the new voters and, predictably, ran best in university towns. (Their highest score, 21 percent, was chalked up in Freiburg, on the edge of the ecologically threatened Black Forest.) Such comparative successes suggested at least two grounds for optimism: the Greens' postindustrial pool of people involved in health and related services was a growing one; the generation gap that had worried the original cadre of leaders as they entered their forties had not materialized—the appeal to the young still held.

As opposed to the inflamed young people of 1968, however, the Greens eschewed violence. Although they might act more often than not outside the parliamentary arena, although one or another Green contingent was demonstrating somewhere nearly every week, their responsible leadership tried—mostly with success—to restrain their militants from pitched battles with the police. Sit-ins and blockings were condoned; striking back was not. A tactic of "gentle provocation": so a not unsympathetic witness has called it.[8]

Among the guiding issues, ecology and the environment naturally came first. After all, the color of the countryside had given the movement its name. And it was the issue with the greatest outreach, even to people otherwise deeply conservative. As inhabitants of an overcrowded, intensely industrialized country, Germans cherished memories of a time long past when their ancestors had dwelt in thick forests; the national culture was "rooted in the myth of the woods." From the Romantic era on, city dwellers had entertained a poetic notion of their remaining forests as a spiritual restorative; for a century and a half at least they had longed to get back to the quiet and the inspiration of open country.

Hence the sense of shock when, in October 1984, the federal minister of economics announced the preliminary results of an investigation into the phenomenon graphically called *Waldsterben*—forest death. Since the turn of the decade, scattered reports of dying trees had been coming thick and fast; by and large industrialists and other "responsible" folk had dismissed them as alarmist. Now the evidence had the ring of the irrefutable. Acid rain from factories (and to a lesser extent emissions from cars) had devastated Germany's forests; in damaged trees the figure of 8 percent in 1982 had risen to 34 percent a year later and to fully half the total by 1984. And the situation was growing worse as one went south: in southern Germany, the more scenic and more wooded part of the country, the number of dead or sick trees rose above the national average; in the state of Baden-Württemberg (which included the Black Forest) it stood at 66 percent.

The official report stated bluntly that nothing short of a full stop to factory emissions could check the ravages in the woodlands.[9] But the federal government and the industrialists alike limited themselves to palliatives. The lesson seemed transparently clear. The ecologically minded had been proved right; the Greens, who for more than a half-decade had been pleading the cause of the forests, had been thoroughly vindicated. Two years later a pair of sensational disasters reinforced the lesson. In April 1986 the breakdown of the nuclear fuel plant at Chernobyl in the Ukraine and the resulting near-panic as contaminated winds blew over Germany could not fail to draw attention to the stand of a party that from the start had opposed the development of such an energy source. The following November a massive spill from a chemical plant at Basel sent a sickening mass of dead fish and eels down the length of the Rhine. By then the election to the Bundestag was only two months away.

On their second great issue—women's rights—the Greens' recommendations sounded less specific and rhetorically diffuse. They also met with greater resistance. Germany's society had remained more blatantly under male control than that of Britain or the United States, and the notion of women as equals was only slowly gaining ground. To the Greens what seemed of primary importance was to hammer on the theme of domination by men in the home. They called not only for ending discrimination in employment and in public life, they called for households in which couples worked as partners. Nor, they believed, should women be forced by male pressure to bear children they neither wanted nor could afford to bring up. In Germany, as in Italy and France, abortion had become a key feminist concern. In the mid-1970s all these countries had legalized it. But of the three laws, the German was the least permissive: prison terms of up to two years threatened both the physician performing the procedure and the woman undergoing it, should they violate any of the meticulously spelled-out limitations with which the right to an abortion was hedged. Quite simply, the Greens demanded an end to such sanctions.[10] And, more simply still, they bore witness to the strength of their belief in equality by sending to the Bundestag in 1987 a majority of women: twenty-five out of a total of forty-four deputies elected.

It was on the third and decisive issue—the question of preserving peace—that the Greens broke with conventional thinking most sharply. Although they frequently squabbled over day-to-day tactics, for the most part they spoke out unequivocally, advocating the eventual dissolution of both NATO and the Warsaw Pact and in the meantime the neutralization of their own country by its withdrawal from the former—in brief, they spoke for unilateral disarmament. For the long run, they envisaged a Europe, East and West, which would be nuclear-free. For the short run, they proposed, as the Welsh had done, sometimes with success, municipal-council resolutions banning nuclear weapons or nuclear industrial installations from individual communities.[11]

How many Germans agreed with them? It was impossible to give a coherent reply to this question. Public-opinion polls offered scant guidance: the answers depended on how the questions were framed, and in the context of what sequence of public events. The matter of peace and of the nuclear threat profoundly perplexed the Germans, as it did their European neighbors. (In the words of one American arms-control specialist, half of them were afraid that the United States would not defend them, half that it would.) Yet the perplexity went deeper than that. It betokened not merely a nation divided in sentiment but individuals divided in their own consciences. Most Germans apparently resorted to double-think: they supported NATO and alignment with the United States as the leaders of the major parties told them to; simultaneously they were all too aware that their country stood exposed as the inevitable battleground of an East-West conflict.

Perhaps the most one can state with any degree of confidence is that the Greens and the German peace movement in general evoked a wider response than was true of any other European country. The October 1983 protest against the stationing of American medium-range missiles gave ample evidence of this. Although the Dutch provided per head of population the largest contingent for the mass demonstrations of that month (comparable to the turnout of the Poles for a papal visit), the West Germans, with nearly a million participants, furnished close to half the Europewide total. As Jürgen Habermas was to note, these "peace demonstrations . . . reached dimensions previously unimaginable in the history of the Federal Republic; they also had a previously unknown quality of, shall we say, disciplined aggressiveness."[12] He might have added that this aggressiveness was tempered by the insistence on a gentler society that had become the leitmotif of the Greens.

When, in the spring of 1983, the newly elected Greens filed into the Bundestag, the sober-minded, sober-suited deputies were in for a shock. The new parliamentarians came with flowers and smiles, clad in blue jeans and similarly outlandish attire. Soon they were addressing their

141

peers with a bluntness to which Bonn was totally unaccustomed. The women deputies among the Greens provoked mutters of "shameless" when they spoke on sexual issues. (One even dared to refer to "penetration" as "the root of the oppression of women.")[13] The sense of incongruity was mutual. The Greens themselves and the majority of the deputies alike wondered what business the newcomers had in being there at all.

Month by month the discrepancies narrowed. While a minority of the Greens carried on in the tradition of vacuous harangues, a larger number settled down to more mundane parliamentary labors on one or another committee. A tenacious lawyer, Otto Schily, who had come a long way since he had served as defense counsel for terrorists, took a leading part in the investigation of a ramifying case of political corruption at the highest levels; by early 1987 three convictions had resulted. A solid and eloquent bookdealer, Joschka Fischer, became the first Green to attain ministerial rank in a state government, that of Hessen, centrally located and left-oriented. His tenure was brief, fourteen months; a shaky coalition of Social Democrats and Greens fell apart, not unexpectedly, over a proposal to construct a nuclear-fuel enterprise, which Fischer, as minister for the environment, refused to countenance. But a precedent had been established.

Schily and Fischer belonged to the Green wing that included most of the Bundestag deputies and had become known as "Realo." The soubriquet betokened their conviction that, with their vote apparently condemned to remain at something like one-tenth of the electorate, they had no choice but to work within the system, preferably alongside the Social Democrats (who in 1987 showed themselves far from eager for such "cohabitation"). This Green electorate, the Realos claimed, in its overwhelming majority, supported a policy of tangible small steps, as did two-thirds of the party members. The Realos' influence was reflected in the program for the election of 1987. Where the 1983 program could be dismissed as a "catalog of good intentions," its successor got down to specifics: proposals to rebuild rather than to tear down old dwellings; to break the "privileged position" of automobiles on streets and highways; to assure a more rational division of labor and a minimum income, this time with a price tag attached.[14]

The opposing wing, the "Fundis" (whose name was likewise self-explanatory), had working for them the long-standing Green distrust of discipline and regularly constituted leadership. Also in their favor was the dominant position in the party's executive they had attained through the fervor of their spokesmen, or better, spokeswomen—fiery, passionate figures such as Jutta Ditfurth or Petra Kelly, determined to resist any compromise with the establishment. This intransigence echoed Max Weber's classic definition of an "ethic of ultimate ends," in which the final goal alone counted, and the ordinary rules of the political game could be dismissed "with a shrug of the shoulders."[15]

Yet to categorize the Fundis in such a fashion would imply consigning the Realos to the opposite realm of an "ethic of responsibility," with all the cool pragmatism and trafficking with "evil" that that entailed. To do so would constitute a grave injustice to men like Schily and Fischer and to the Green militants who looked to them for tactical direction. No less than the Fundis did the Realos aim at a new type of society, drawing its strength from local initiatives and ever on the alert for abuses of power. They simply accepted the fact of their minority situation in the Federal Republic— nothing more damaging than that. In common with the soberer heads among the Welsh nationalists or the veterans of Poland's Solidarity, they realized full well how long a march they had before them until anything resembling the Europe of their dreams could materialize; in the meantime the establishments they confronted held nearly all the cards. In this sobriety the Realos epitomized the hard-won wisdom of those who had learned the lesson of 1968.

Another Fin de Siècle?

B y 1987 the twenty-first century was in sight. It might be only rarely, as at the Cavtat meeting of socialist intellectuals, that the approaching end of one millennium and the advent of another were explicitly invoked, but the thought hovered ever more insistently in the back of people's minds. For two decades it had been apparent that the post-Second World War era was over. By 1987 the span of time that had elapsed since the conflict's close had more than doubled that of the interwar years. In West and East alike, those wearied by the stale repetitiousness of postwar ethico-political routines were on the lookout for new formulations, new procedures. Germany's Greens offered the most engaging Western example; Poland's Solidarity and Russia's Gorbachev, in utterly contrasting fashions, demonstrated that the East too had begun to stir.

Centuries, millennia: these are of course no more than arbitrary demarcations imposed by unquestioned convention. But by their very obviousness and universality they acquire an emotional and cultural content of their own, a capacity to influence the way in which even ordinary folk reckon up their lives. So had it been throughout the Western world in the late 1880s; so is it today throughout the planet. Once we begin to make the comparison, extraordinary juxtapositions spring to mind: with the suppression of the insurrectionary spirit

(1871, 1968), conservative rule in most countries for most of the time; with the onset of economic uncertainty (1873, 1973) and shattered illusions about uninterrupted expansion, a closing of the ranks among the propertied classes; with a "long peace" taken for granted, a shift of anxiety away from Europe and toward intractable struggles or rivalries in Asia and Africa, plus an arms race generating its own momentum.

A century ago, the French found an expression for the mood of the era, and the words *fin de siècle,* untranslated, caught the imagination elsewhere. What was meant by the expression was far from clear; its connotations were protean. As often as not, it suggested weariness or boredom with the century that was "expiring," and a corresponding excitement about the new one on the verge of birth. Trepidation and hope oscillated in uneasy balance: social thinkers wallowed in foreboding; the common citizen celebrated the glorious future that was "dawning." In this case the prophets of disaster proved the more farseeing: the promise of a new century of peace and social justice gradually collapsed as one disappointment followed another. (Or perhaps the public morale of Europeans never recovered from the trauma of the First World War.) The second time round—in the late 1980s—we hear little of promise, but instead, a lugubrious enumeration of approaching crises, of insoluble difficulties looming ahead. Such modest expectations epitomize the disabused temper bequeathed by the waning century.

Where do the protagonists of this book fit among these diverse moods of anticipation? A number of them saw no point in trying to reckon with future uncertainties; they were far too busy with the here and now. Foreign workers expended nearly all their energies in scratching out a living or holding onto the rudiments of personal dignity. Their literary defender, Heinrich Böll, although sustained by the vision of a gentler society, became increasingly absorbed in

145

he day-by-day battle against the injustice he saw about him. Others frankly, unapologetically, looked backward. The autonomists of France and Britain's "Celtic fringes" cultivated the traces of a past that was disappearing before their eyes. Novelists sounded the nostalgic note—Michel Tournier and Milan Kundera with self-irony and without bitterness, Alexander Solzhenitsyn in tones of ringing denunciation. Those who looked forward talked less of a new century than of a new type of relations among human beings, of a protracted process of cumulative change which had little or nothing to do with a conventional demarcation of time.

Could they be called postmodern? Possibly—in view of their wariness, their distaste for established criteria, whether political or rhetorical, that I have called "sophisticated." Had they understood what the currently modish term meant (its meaning seemed clear only in the realm of architecture), they would have been put off by its unabashed eclecticism, its penchant for pastiche, irreverent or elegant as the case might be, and the way it "impudently" embraced "the language of commerce and the commodity."[1] On this score Jürgen Habermas was unequivocal. Taking his cue from Jacques Derrida's "capering deconstructivism," he ticked off the manifestations of the cultural universe that postmodernism seemed inclined to accept or even applaud: "the banal" coalescing with "the unreal," a blending of "hellenistic . . . customs . . . with high-tech style, . . . the ruins of popular cultures" coexisting "with the highly personalized, consumeristically polished bizarre," the "refuse dumps of civilization . . . camouflaged with plastic."[2] Habermas was not alone in finding the contemporary artistic temper repellent; countless others who shared his deep seriousness were inclined to shrug their shoulders at postmodernism and to pass it by.

Another aspect to the phenomenon could not be dismissed so easily. Jean-François Lyotard, Derrida's heir, was its most influential expositor. For Lyotard the postmodern meant something more devastating than mere cultural promiscuity. It cast into obsolescence the traditional notion of *Bildung,* of the patient, loving transformation of human raw material into an educated citizenry; "quantities of information, . . . translatable into computer language," could do service instead. This new variety of knowledge, Lyotard maintained, "in the form of an informational commodity indispensable to productive power," was already "a major—perhaps *the* major—stake in . . . worldwide competition." It was "conceivable that the nation-states" would "one day fight for control of information, just as they battled in the past for control over territory, and afterwards for control of access to and exploitation of raw materials and cheap labor."[3]

By this eccentric route Lyotard managed to link postmodernism with the world of computers and information banks. Here too our protagonists failed to figure. If theirs was still the discriminating, carefully articulated cultural world of the "modern," it was also a world in which novel information techniques seldom played a role (as they did in Solidarity's astute exploitation of up-to-date communications systems and the foreign mass media's hunger for news). Most of the time the people discussed in this book preferred—or were driven by necessity—to fall back on simpler, more personal methods, on the tried-and-true. If they anticipated some cultural awakening for the twenty-first century, they envisioned it in the guise of a humanism that structuralism, deconstruction, and the postmodern had abandoned. They could scarcely imagine that *these* were anything more than transitory manifestations or false dawns.

In one respect, however, writers like Lyotard were abreast of reality and our protagonists were not. The latter lived and worked in a number of little worlds, on the margin of the major global spectacle. The "great world" of multinational corporations, of an interlocking military-industrial complex nearly universal in scope, might give them pause, but they found no way to cope with it. Were they pygmies, then, when

147

pitted against the giant forces which technology had unleashed? Were they merely heeding their own dreams, oblivious to the thunder of the overwhelming realities which were shaking the planet? Is it wrong to rank them as exponents of what was new and heartening in Europe's political culture of the 1970s and 1980s?

"Speak truth to power": this fundamental Quaker maxim reminds us of how down the centuries ethically minded people have marshaled their puny resources against establishments of all descriptions. The individuals, the groups, with whom we have been dealing had in common a resolute moral sense. There was nothing bombastic about it, just as there was no trace of violence. Most of the time it was laced with humor, even self-deprecation. The men and women who thought otherwise bore witness to their beliefs with quiet stoicism in the face of almost unremitting disappointment. Gently, insistently, they told Europe's conservative rulers the things that those in power least liked to hear. In their unwearying reiteration of truths they held to be self-evident, in the inventiveness they displayed in proposing alternative patterns of thought and action, they were engaged in an ongoing process of "subversion in a minor key."[4]

It seldom occurred to them that their basic beliefs required precise definition. The theologians who argued with the Pope, no less than the Russians who took a stand for human rights, entertained few if any doubts about the rightness of their cause. In this certainty lay the secret (if such it could be called) of their success in reaching out beyond the confines of those who thought as they did: by the serenity with which they entertained their convictions, they won the grudging admiration of their enemies and shook up the complacency of the rest. These convictions amounted to a plea for common decency, for justice, for compassion, backed up as a last resort by nonviolent civil disobedience—above all, a plea to their fellow citizens to curb the impersonal powers that ruled their lives and thereby to reassert control by human beings over their own destinies. The goal necessarily entailed a rebellious temper, a stance of irreverent defiance, but not the ruthless zeal of revolutionaries. On the contrary, its stress on the person-to-person relations of a bygone day might well reassure those who were genuine conservatives rather than mere exploiters of conservative rhetoric to manipulative ends.

The foregoing may suggest that our protagonists, however few in number, spoke, like the German Greens, to a passive constituency with wide if uncertain boundaries. On three matters in particular they could evoke deep-running sympathy.

The first, largely a Western phenomenon, but discernible in the East also, was the impending "formation of a *two-thirds society.*" Habermas had touched on it without giving it a name; so had Pietro Ingrao at Cavtat. In societies whose conservative leaders unashamedly favored individual ownership at the expense of community values, those leaders were proving "willing to accept the social decline (not the absolute pauperization) of the weakest third" of their citizenry: "the unemployed, the odd-jobbers, the elderly of the lower classes, the migrant workers, the physically and mentally handicapped, the teenagers" unable to "find their way into the job market."[5] The other two-thirds, for the present at least, seemed content with the measure of security they enjoyed. When reminded of the plight of their less fortunate countrymen, they usually looked the other way. In the two-thirds society, compassion was in short supply; it received scant encouragement from on high. But such might not forever be the case. The sufferings of the marginalized, the squalor of decaying inner cities, were already alarming those who had eyes to see. And when the hour of a renewed human solidarity should strike, a devoted cohort of advocates stood ready to help redirect the priorities of populations awakened at last to the ravages of unbridled egoism.

The people already half-awake generally looked beyond their own national frontiers. They realized that the social evils they had discovered at home were echoed abroad by similar evils. In common with those who had originally sounded the alarm, people of this sort tended to be "good Europeans." (We earlier noted how Welsh and Bretons and the like spoke not only for loyalty to a historic culture within the nation-state but for a wider loyalty beyond that state.) To be a good European once meant to favor the integration of the West. By the 1980s it meant to call for a reunited continent. This was the second matter on which our protagonists could reckon on growing support.

Here, however, as with the third, that of the nuclear menace, the demand for reknitting ties between East and West was undercut by a tragic misunderstanding, "a gulf of mutual incomprehension," more particularly between West Germans and Poles. Solidarity and the Greens (or the German peace movement in general) spoke radically divergent languages. For the former, top priority went to liberation from tyranny; for the latter, to combatting the threat of nuclear war.[6] The same divergence could be noted more widely among populations on one side or the other of the ideological divide.

Yet, as the Polish historian Bronisław Geremek had suggested, the two matters were in fact linked: progress on the one implied a corresponding progress on the other. Eastern Europeans could not expect to gain any substantial measure of national and personal freedom unless and until the leaders of the Soviet Union found reason to relax their posture of armed vigilance. This most people dimly understood, however infrequently they might speak of it. This our protagonists also understood, however varied the emphases they placed on peace or on liberation. This Pope John Paul II

150

understood as well—hence his veiled but persistent pursuit of his own version of *Ostpolitik.*

In June 1987 the original architect of *Ostpolitik,* Willy Brandt, retired from the chairmanship of the party he had served so long and so well. In his farewell address he reminded fellow Social Democrats of a few basic truths they were in danger of forgetting. Piecemeal arms-control arrangements between the Soviet Union and the United States he found insufficient for the "assured world peace" to which he aspired. In similiar vein he warned his colleagues against a narrowness of vision that in practice excluded from consideration so many of the marginal. His party, he contended, needed "the critical sympathy of so-called outsiders"; it needed "uncomfortable" people, those who thought "at cross purposes," "birds in motley," who on occasion made fun of politicians like himself. (A lack of humor he reckoned "no key to success.")[7] His tone suggested that Brandt was speaking of our protagonists and their like.

In conclusion he quoted the last words Léon Blum "put on paper": "I believe it because I hope for it." In a spirit such as this the men and women of good will and of good hope whose fortunes we have been pursuing stood ready to welcome the new century.

Notes

one. "The Moral Equivalent of War"

1. Kazimierz Brandys, *A Warsaw Diary, 1978–1981,* trans. Richard Lourie (New York: Random House, 1983), p. 43.
2. Arthur Marwick, *British Society since 1945* (London: Penguin, 1982), p. 129; John Ardagh, *France in the 1980s* (London: Penguin, 1982), p. 539.
3. E. P. Thompson, *The Making of the English Working Class* (New York: Pantheon, 1963), p. 13.
4. Fritz Stern, "Reflections on the International Student Movement," *The American Scholar,* 40 (Winter 1970), 126–127.
5. The foregoing quotations are from the introduction to the meticulous and exhaustive collection edited by Alain Schnapp and Pierre Vidal-Naquet, *Journal de la commune étudiante: Textes et documents, novembre 1967–juin 1968* (Paris: Seuil, 1969), pp. 35, 51.
6. Raymond Aron, *La révolution introuvable* (Paris: Fayard, 1968), trans. Gordon Clough, *The Elusive Revolution: Anatomy of a Student Revolt* (New York: Praeger, 1969), pp. 15, 19, 21, 24, 25.
7. Karl Heinz Bohrer, "The Three Cultures," in Jürgen Habermas, ed., *Stichworte zur 'Geistigen Situation der Zeit'* (Frankfurt: Suhrkamp, 1979), abridged trans. Andrew Buchwalter, *Observations on "The Spiritual Situation of the Age": Contemporary German Perspectives* (Cambridge, Mass.: MIT Press, 1984), pp. 125–126.
8. Stephen Spender, *The Year of the Young Rebels* (New York: Random House, 1969), pp. 76–77.
9. Karen Dawisha, *The Kremlin and the Prague Spring* (Berkeley and Los Angeles: University of California Press, 1984), pp. 239, 285–287, 300.
10. H. Gordon Skilling, *Czechoslovakia's Interrupted Revolution* (Princeton: Princeton University Press, 1976), pp. 349–350.
11. The text of Two Thousand Words is published in Robin Alison Remington, ed., *Winter in Prague: Documents on Czechoslovak Communism in Crisis* (Cambridge, Mass.: MIT Press, 1969), pp. 196–202; that of Dubček's July 18 speech as an appendix to Philip Windsor and Adam Roberts, *Czechoslovakia 1968: Reform, Repression and Resistance* (New York: Columbia University Press, 1969), pp. 169–173.
12. Skilling, *Interrupted Revolution,* pp. 372, 514–515.
13. Ibid., pp. 657, 844.
14. Obviously this criterion excludes small groups dedicated to terrorism or violence.

15. Brandys, *Warsaw Diary,* p. 238; Philip Roth, "Afterward: A Talk with the Author," in Milan Kundera, *The Book of Laughter and Forgetting,* trans. Michael Henry Heim (London: Penguin, 1981), p. 230. Compare Kundera's statement "Study Poland! After 1945, Poland became the real center of Europe" in Jordan Elgrably, "Conversations with Milan Kundera," *Salmagundi* (Winter 1987), p. 15; and his "vision of Europe as a culture, not a territory" in Charles Molesworth, "Kundera and *The Book,*" ibid., p. 66.

two. The Parisian Scene: The Return of the Novel

1. John Sturrock, ed., *Structuralism and Since: From Lévi-Strauss to Derrida* (Oxford: Oxford University Press, 1979), pp. 1–2.
2. François Furet, *L'atelier de l'histoire* (Paris: Flammarion, 1982), trans. Jonathan Mandelbaum, *In the Workshop of History* (Chicago: University of Chicago Press, 1984), pp. 38–39.
3. Sturrock, *Structuralism and Since,* pp. 13, 15; Pamela Major-Poetzl, *Michel Foucault's Archaeology of Western Culture: Toward a New Science of History* (Chapel Hill: University of North Carolina Press, 1983), p. 166.
4. Stuart Schneiderman, *Jacques Lacan: The Death of an Intellectual Hero* (Cambridge, Mass.: Harvard University Press, 1983), pp. 16, 132–133, 157, 181, a unique first-hand account with the ring of authenticity. For examples of Lacan's reflections on death, see *Le Séminaire de Jacques Lacan, Livre XI* (Paris: Seuil, 1973), trans. Alan Sheridan, *The Four Fundamental Concepts of Psycho-Analysis* (New York: Norton, 1978), pp. 223, 257.
5. Michel Foucault, *Les mots et les choses: Une archéologie des sciences humaines* (Paris: Gallimard, 1966), trans. Alan Sheridan-Smith, *The Order of Things: An Archaeology of the Human Sciences* (New York: Random House, 1970), p. 387.
6. These shifts are lucidly aligned by Jonathan Culler in *Roland Barthes* (New York: Oxford University Press, 1983).
7. Roland Barthes, *Mythologies* (Paris: Seuil, 1957), abridged trans. Annette Lavers under same title (New York: Hill and Wang, 1972), p. 155, *Leçon inaugurale . . .* (Paris: Seuil, 1978), trans. in Susan Sontag, ed., *A Barthes Reader* (New York: Hill and Wang, 1982), pp. 459–460, 472.
8. Ibid., pp. 475–476; Foucault, *Order of Things,* p. 326.
9. André Glucksmann, *Les maîtres penseurs* (Paris: Grasset, 1977), trans. Brian Pearce, *The Master Thinkers* (New York: Harper & Row, 1980), pp. 269, 286.

10. Bernard-Henri Lévy, *La barbarie à visage humain* (Paris: Grasset, 1977), trans. George Holoch, *Barbarism with a Human Face* (New York: Harper & Row, 1979), pp. 56, 67, 112, 197.
11. Among others, in H. Stuart Hughes, *The Obstructed Path* (New York: Harper & Row, 1968).
12. Michel Tournier, *Vendredi ou les limbes du Pacifique* (Paris: Gallimard, 1967), trans. Norman Denny, *Friday* (London: Collins, 1969), ch. 8.
13. Michel Tournier, *Le Roi des Aulnes* (Paris: Gallimard, 1970), trans. Barbara Bray, *The Ogre* (Garden City, N.Y.: Doubleday, 1972), p. 370.
14. Michel Tournier, *Le vent Paraclet* (Paris: Gallimard, 1977), pp. 7, 113. Note the religious connotations of the title ("The Breath of the Holy Spirit") in this volume of autobiographical essays and reflections.
15. Ibid., pp. 21, 62–65.
16. Michel Tournier, *Gaspard, Melchior & Balthazar* (Paris: Gallimard, 1980), trans. Ralph Mannheim, *The Four Wise Men* (Garden City, N.Y.: Doubleday, 1982).
17. Tournier, *Vent Paraclet,* pp. 69, 71–75, 105.
18. Ibid., pp. 89–90, 110–111.
19. Tournier, *Ogre,* p. 338.
20. Tournier, *Vent Paraclet,* pp. 221–222, 295.
21. Ibid., pp. 88 and n2 (for an example of the author's occasional outrageousness of expression).
22. Ibid., pp. 114–115, 130, 179–180, 195, 205.
23. Ibid., pp. 146, 246. See also two interviews—Jacqueline Piatier, "Où nous mène Michel Tournier?" *Le Monde,* May 27, 1983; Jürg Altwegg, "Der einsame Erlkönig," *Die Zeit,* 38 (Oct. 28, 1983).
24. Tournier, *Ogre,* p. 94, *Vent Paraclet,* p. 27; Piatier, "Où nous mène?"
25. Tournier, *Vent Paraclet,* pp. 56, 125; Altwegg, "Einsamer Erlkönig."
26. Philip Roth, "Afterword: A Talk with the Author," in Milan Kundera, *The Book of Laughter and Forgetting,* trans. Michael Henry Heim (London: Penguin, 1981), p. 231; Olga Carlisle, "A Talk with Milan Kundera," *The New York Times Magazine,* May 19, 1985, to which one may add the *cri de coeur* "I'll never have the strength to emigrate from Paris to Prague": Jordan Elgrably, "Conversations with Milan Kundera," *Salmagundi* (Winter 1987), p. 12.
27. Milan Kundera, *The Unbearable Lightness of Being,* trans. Michael Henry Heim (New York: Harper & Row, 1985), pp. 72–73, 222–223.
28. Milan Kundera, *The Joke,* trans. Michael Henry Heim (London: Penguin, 1983), p. 76, *Laughter and Forgetting,* pp. 8, 62–63, 65–66, *Unbearable Lightness,* p. 257.

29. Ibid., p. 223.

30. Roth, "Afterword," p. 235; Kundera, *Joke,* pp. 244, 261–262.

31. Ibid., Author's Preface, p. xii.

32. Ibid.

33. Tournier, *Vent Paraclet,* pp. 146–147.

34. Ibid., pp. 198–199; Milan Kundera, "Man Thinks, God Laughs," *The New York Review of Books,* 32 (June 13, 1985).

three. The Torment of a Foreign Underclass

1. Michel Tournier, *Le vent Paraclet* (Paris: Gallimard, 1977), p. 236. Eight years later he made a young North African worker the protagonist of his novel *La goutte d'or* (Paris: Gallimard, 1985), trans. Barbara Wright, *The Golden Droplet* (New York: Doubleday, 1987).

2. Stephen Castles (with Heather Booth and Tina Wallace), *Here for Good: Western Europe's New Ethnic Minorities* (London and Sydney: Pluto, 1984), p. 124.

3. Stephen Castles and Godula Kosack, *Immigrant Workers and Class Structure in Western Europe,* 2nd ed. (Oxford: Oxford University Press, 1985), p. 492.

4. Ibid., p. 8.

5. Friedrich Heckmann, *Die Bundesrepublik: Ein Einwanderungsland? Zur Soziologie der Gastarbeiterbevölkerung als Einwandererminorität* (Stuttgart: Klett-Cotta, 1981), pp. 159, 177, 222.

6. Regulation cited in Castles et al., *Here for Good,* p. 77.

7. Castles and Kosack, *Immigrant Workers,* pp. 342–343.

8. Ibid., pp. 365–366, 502–503; Castles et al., *Here for Good,* pp. 165–166, 188.

9. Ibid., pp. 175, 186.

10. Heckmann, *Einwanderungsland?,* pp. 208–210.

11. Robert Solé, "Portugais de France: La face cachée de l'immigration," *Le Monde,* Oct. 19, 1985.

12. Ann Cornelisen, *Strangers and Pilgrims: The Last Italian Migration* (New York: Holt, Rinehart and Winston, 1980), pp. 166, 174, 292, 302. For a bleaker view of the Italians as oppressed (but also more *menschlich* than the Germans), see Anna Picardi-Montesardo, *Die Gastarbeiter in der Literatur der Bundesrepublik Deutschland* (Berlin: Express, 1985), pp. 51, 66–69, 76–79, 87–88.

13. Bernard Stasi, *L'Immigration: Une chance pour la France* (Paris: Laffont, 1984), pp. 17, 63–66, 104.

14. Ibid., pp. 67–68, 101, 106, 145.

15. Heckmann, *Einwanderungsland?*, p. 220; Castles et al., *Here for Good,* pp. 100, 138.
16. Gerhard Spörl, "Ali, der gute Deutsche," *Die Zeit* 41 (Feb. 13, 1986). Picardi-Montesardo (pp. 106–109) documents a German concern with the fragmentary writings of foreign workers as early as 1980.
17. Roland Kirbach, "Fakir Baykurt: Von Anatolien nach Duisburg," *Die Zeit,* 40 (Aug. 2, 1985).
18. Fakir Baykurt, *Nachtschicht: Und andere Erzählungen aus Deutschland,* trans. Helga Dağyeli-Bohne and Yildirim Dağyeli (Zurich: Unionsverlag, 1984), pp. 16–20, 63–67, 74–77, 101, 105, 112–115.
19. The title story, "Nachtschicht," Ibid., pp. 82–94.
20. Castles and Kosack, *Immigrant Workers,* p. 503.
21. Hakki Keskin, "Diese Ausländerpolitik fördert Ausländerhass," *Die Zeit,* 41 (Jan. 24, 1986).

four. The Reassertion of Historic Cultures: The Case of Wales

1. Morvan Lebesque, *Comment peut-on être breton?* (Paris: Seuil, 1970), pp. 199, 202–203.
2. Suzanne Berger, "Bretons, Basques, Scots, and Other European Nations," *Journal of Interdisciplinary History,* 3 (1972): 168.
3. Auguste Brun, *Parlers régionaux: France dialectale et unité française* (Paris & Toulouse: Didier, 1946), pp. 67–68, 76–78, 87.
4. See, for example, Lebesque, *Comment peut-on?,* p. 215.
5. Jack E. Reece, *The Bretons against France: Ethnic Minority Nationalism in Twentieth-Century Brittany* (Chapel Hill: University of North Carolina Press, 1977), pp. 87–88, 167.
6. Jan Morris, *The Matter of Wales: Epic Views of a Small Country* (Oxford and New York: Oxford University Press, 1984), pp. 72–73, 158. Despite its impressionistic approach and high-flown style, this work is a mine of information.
7. On all the above, see Kenneth O. Morgan, *Rebirth of a Nation: Wales, 1880–1980* (New York: Oxford University Press, University of Wales Press, 1981), the authoritative account.
8. "The pied pipers speak Welsh," *The Economist,* August 6, 1983; Morris, *Matter of Wales,* pp. 418–419.
9. Kenneth O. Morgan in *The Times Literary Supplement,* March 2, 1984.
10. Glyn Jones, *The Dragon Has Two Tongues: Essays on Anglo-Welsh Writers and Writing* (London: Dent, 1968), pp. 14, 44, 206, 208.
11. Gwyn Thomas, *A Welsh Eye* (London: Hutchinson, 1964), pp. 24, 32–33.

12. Morris, *Matter of Wales,* p. 144.
13. For the functioning of these institutions, see James G. Kellas, *The Scottish Political System,* 3rd ed. (Cambridge: Cambridge University Press, 1984).
14. I am well aware that to this day spoken Scottish English differs perceptibly from southern English usage in vocabulary and turn of phrase and that a handful of authors continue to write in full-blown Scots.
15. Kellas, *Scottish Political System,* p. 138.
16. Morgan, *Rebirth of a Nation,* p. 405.
17. For the earlier view, see Patricia Elton Mayo, *The Roots of Identity: Three National Movements in Contemporary European Politics* (London: Allen Lane, 1974), p. 154.
18. Ibid., p. 91.

five. The Pope and His Antagonists

1. Norman St. John-Stevas, *The Agonizing Choice: Birth Control, Religion and the Law* (Bloomington and London: Indiana University Press, 1971), p. 7.
2. Peter Hebblethwaite, *The Runaway Church* (London: Collins, 1975), p. 86. The liveliest and best informed account of this and subsequent Vatican doings available in English is to be found here and in its four sequels: *The Year of Three Popes* (London: Collins, 1978); *The New Inquisition? Schillebeeckx and Küng* (London: Collins, 1980); *Synod Extraordinary: The Inside Story of the Rome Synod November–December 1985* (Garden City, N.Y.: Doubleday, 1986); *In the Vatican* (London: Sidgwick and Jackson, 1986).
3. Conor Cruise O'Brien, "The Liberal Pope," *The New York Review of Books,* 32 (Oct. 10, 1985).
4. For John Paul II's background, education, and attitude toward the Council, see John Whale, ed., *The Pope from Poland: An Assessment* (London: Collins, 1980), pp. 14–19, 50–51, 229.
5. Ibid., pp. 257–259; Philippe Pons, "Le Vatican saisi par la géopolitique," *Le Monde,* Aug. 9, 1985.
6. For the salient biographical points, see Leonard Swidler, ed., *Küng in Conflict* (Garden City, N.Y.: Doubleday, 1981), pp. 1–4.
7. Hans Küng, *Infallible? An Inquiry,* trans. Edward Quinn (Garden City, N.Y.: Doubleday, 1971), pp. 81, 86, 198.
8. Hans Küng, "Warum ich trotzdem noch katholisch bin," *Die Zeit,* 38 (Nov. 4, 1983), "Die alte Inquisition ist tot, es lebe die neue," *Die Zeit,* 40 (Oct. 11, 1985).

9. Again for biographical data, see Robert Schreiter, ed., *The Schille-beeckx Reader* (New York: Crossroad, 1984), pp. 1–24.

10. For the passages cited, see Edward Schillebeeckx, *Jesus: An Experiment in Christology,* trans. Hubert Hoskins (London: Collins, 1979), pp. 380, 544; for the conversation of 1979 in Rome, see Hebblethwaite, *New Inquisition?,* ch. 4.

11. Ibid., p. 124.

12. Hebblethwaite, *Synod Extraordinary,* p. 45.

13. See the interview with Leonardo Boff in *Le Monde,* March 22, 1985, and his book *Church, Charism, and Power: Liberation Theology and the Institutional Church,* trans. John W. Diercksmeier (London: SCM, 1986).

14. Pons, "Vatican saisi par la géopolitique."

15. Kazimierz Brandys, *A Warsaw Diary, 1978–1981,* trans. Richard Lourie (New York: Random House, 1983), pp. 67, 157. For a full account of the visit, see Whale, *Pope from Poland,* ch. 6.

six. The Sixteen Months of Solidarity

1. For the foregoing paragraphs I am drawing on the exhaustive account of a major participant, Jan Jósef Lipski, *KOR: A History of the Workers' Defense Committee in Poland, 1976–1981,* trans. Olga Amsterdamska and Gene M. Moore (Berkeley, Los Angeles, and London: University of California Press, 1985), pp. 44–45, 70–76, 208–212, 279–285, 385–386, 453–454, 458.

2. Timothy Garton Ash, *The Polish Revolution: Solidarity* (New York: Vintage, 1985), p. 30.

3. Leszek Kołakowski, "The Intelligentsia," in Abraham Brumberg, ed., *Poland: Genesis of a Revolution* (New York: Vintage, 1983), p. 65.

4. Ash, *Polish Revolution,* p. 231; the text of the Gdańsk Agreement is published as an appendix to Brumberg, *Poland,* pp. 285–295.

5. Adam Michnik, *Letters from Prison and Other Essays,* trans. Maya Latynski (Berkeley, Los Angeles, and London: University of California Press, 1985), pp. 29, 31.

6. Kazimierz Brandys, *A Warsaw Diary, 1978–1981,* trans. Richard Lourie (New York: Random House, 1983), p. 232.

7. See the paragraphs of autobiography in Michnik, *Letters from Prison,* pp. 202–203.

8. Ash, *Polish Revolution,* p. 143.

9. Flora Lewis, "A Pole in Moscow," *The New York Times,* March 9, 1986.

10. Mieczysław F. Rakowski, *Ein schwieriger Dialog: Aufzeichnungen zu*

Ereignissen in Polen, 1981–1984, trans. Armin Th. Dross (Düsseldorf and Vienna: Econ, 1985), p. 22. This diary, despite the gaps and passages of special pleading to be expected, provides the best glimpse available into the thought processes of those trying to ride out the storm.

11. Ibid., pp. 35, 44–45, 73, 92.
12. Ash, *Polish Revolution,* pp. 212–214, 237.
13. On this point, surprisingly, Ash, *Polish Revolution,* pp. 225, 260–261, and Rakowski, *Schwieriger Dialog,* p. 101, are in substantial agreement.
14. Michnik, *Letters from Prison,* pp. 29, 89–90.
15. Ash, *Polish Revolution,* p. 300. The figure is from the Polish Helsinki Watch Committee.
16. Michnik, *Letters from Prison,* p. 77.
17. Ash, *Polish Revolution,* pp. 351, 353–354.
18. "Life in the other Poland," *The Economist,* Aug. 3, 1985.
19. Michnik, *Letters from Prison,* pp. 107, 110. See also J. T., "Realpolitik—The Politics of Realities," in Brumberg, *Poland,* pp. 267, 271.
20. Interview in *Le Monde,* Aug. 31, 1985. Two years later the themes of refusing to "desert," of not giving up, of lasting it out, suffused the Pope's once again scarcely veiled references to Solidarity on his third trip to Poland, as they did the autobiographical reflections of Lech Wałęsa, *A Way of Hope,* (New York: Holt, 1987).

seven. The Frustration of Soviet Dissent

1. Ludmilla Alexeyeva, *Soviet Dissent: Contemporary Movements for National, Religious, and Human Rights,* trans. Carol Pearce and John Glad (Middletown, Conn.: Wesleyan University Press, 1985), p. 9. This fundamental account, by a former participant now living in exile, has the added virtue of giving full attention to non–Russian movements.
2. Donald R. Shanor, *Behind the Lines: The Private War against Soviet Censorship* (New York: St. Martin's, 1985), p. 159.
3. Gayle Durham Hollander, "Political Communication and Dissent in the Soviet Union," in Rudolf L. Tökés, ed., *Dissent in the USSR: Politics, Ideology, and People* (Baltimore and London: Johns Hopkins University Press, 1975), pp. 241–243, 254.
4. Ibid., pp. 248, 251; Alexeyeva, *Soviet Dissent,* p. 307.
5. Hollander, "Political Communication and Dissent," p. 246.
6. Vladimir Bukovsky, quoted in Alexeyeva, *Soviet Dissent,* p. 12.
7. Joshua Rubenstein, *Soviet Dissidents: Their Struggle for Human Rights,*

2nd ed. (Boston: Beacon, 1985), p. 320. Although less complete than Alexeyeva's, this account has the advantages of a chronological organization and a fluent style.

8. Aleksandr I. Solzhenitsyn, *The Gulag Archipelago, 1918–1956: An Experiment in Literary Investigation,* trans. Thomas P. Whitney, II (New York: Harper & Row, 1975), p. 214.

9. Michael Scammell, *Solzhenitsyn: A Biography* (New York and London: Norton, 1984), p. 25. For most of what follows I am relying on this scrupulous and altogether admirable work.

10. Solzhenitsyn, *Gulag Archipelago,* II, 617.

11. Scammell, *Solzhenitsyn,* pp. 238, 270.

12. Ibid., p. 339.

13. Ibid., pp. 384, 449, 485. Alexander Solzhenitsyn, *One Day in the Life of Ivan Denisovich,* trans. Max Hayward and Ronald Hingley (New York: Praeger, 1963), p. 203.

14. Aleksandr I. Solzhenitsyn, *The First Circle,* trans. Thomas P. Whitney (New York: Harper & Row, 1968), pp. 116, 345, 553. The full version, which to date has not appeared in English, was published in Russian in Paris in 1978.

15. Solzhenitsyn, *Gulag Archipelago,* II, 7, 208, 490, 601.

16. Ibid., pp. 152–153.

17. Alexander Solzhenitsyn, *August 1914,* trans. Michael Glenny (London: Bodley Head, 1972), *Lenin in Zürich,* trans. H. T. Willetts (London: Bodley Head, 1976). The first of these was incorporated into a much expanded version under the same title (and as the first "knot" of the epic), published in Russian in Paris in 1983.

18. Scammell, *Solzhenitsyn,* p. 736; Jutta Scherrer, "Exil im Exil: Ein Tag im Leben des Alexander Issajewitsch," *Die Zeit,* 39 (Feb. 3, 1984).

19. Notably in his commencement address at Harvard University in June 1978. The text was published in *Harvard Magazine,* July–August 1978, pp. 21–26.

20. Theodore Friedgut, "The Democratic Movement: Dimensions and Perspectives," in Tökés, *Dissent in the USSR,* p. 118.

21. Alexeyeva, *Soviet Dissent,* pp. 268, 294.

22. Ibid., pp. 291, 293–294, 329–330, 335–338; Rubenstein, *Soviet Dissidents,* ch. 7.

23. Ibid., pp. 328–329.

24. For an authoritative and lively account, see Mark Hopkins, *Russia's Underground Press: The Chronicle of Current Events* (New York: Praeger, 1983), pp. 21, 28–29, 64, 88–89, 116, 120, 126, 148.

25. For the highlights of Andrei Sakharov's early biography, see the introduction by one of the editors, Alfred Friendly, Jr., to the collec-

tion of statements *Alarm and Hope* (New York: Vintage, 1978), pp. xii–xv; for a harrowing account of his banishment from Moscow, see the interview with an old friend, Natalya Viktorovna Hesse, "The Sakharovs in Gorky," *The New York Review of Books*, 31 (April 12, 1984); for a partial list of the astonishing number of statements he succeeded in issuing from there, see Rubenstein, *Soviet Dissidents*, pp. 290–292.

26. "Progress, Coexistence, and Intellectual Freedom," in the collection of Andrei Sakharov's writings entitled *Sakharov Speaks* (New York: Knopf, 1974), pp. 37, 104–105, 117.

27. Notably in *My Country and the World*, trans. Guy V. Daniels (New York: Knopf, 1975). For Sakharov's qualifying statements, see *Alarm and Hope*, pp. 17, 109.

28. Shanor, *Behind the Lines*, p. 125.

29. Friedgut, "Democratic Movement," p. 131; George Feifer, "No Protest: The Case of the Passive Majority," in Tökés, *Dissent in the USSR*, pp. 426–427.

30. Sergei Grigoryants, quoted in Alexeyeva, *Soviet Dissent*, p. 389; Rubenstein, *Soviet Dissidents*, p. 310.

31. Hopkins, *Russia's Underground Press*, pp. 111, 155–156.

32. Donald Fanger, "A Change of Venue: Russian Journals of the Emigration," *The Times Literary Supplement*, Nov. 21, 1986.

33. Geoffrey Hosking in ibid., Dec. 6, 1985; foreword by John Updike to Yuri Trifonov, *Another Life* and *The House on the Embankment*, trans. Michael Glenny (New York: Simon and Schuster, 1986), pp. 1–8.

34. Yuri Trifonov, *The Old Man*, trans. Jacqueline Edwards and Mitchell Schneider (New York: Simon and Schuster, 1984).

35. For a curriculum vitae, see the introduction to Roy Medvedev, *On Socialist Democracy*, trans. Ellen de Kadt (New York: Knopf, 1975), p. viii.

36. Ibid., pp. 56–58, 101, 308.

37. Roy Medvedev, *On Soviet Dissent: Interviews with Piero Ostellino*, trans. William A. Packer and George Saunders (New York: Columbia University Press, 1980), pp. 90, 127, 147.

eight. Democratic Socialism: North and South

1. Roy Medvedev, *Leninism and Western Socialism*, trans. A. D. P. Briggs (London: Verso, 1981), pp. 25, 82, 200, 271, 293; italics in original.

2. Martin Jay, *Marxism and Totality: The Adventures of a Concept from Lukács to Habermas* (Berkeley and Los Angeles: University of California Press, 1984), p. 535.

3. Notably with his editorship of *Stichworte zur 'Geistigen Situation der Zeit'* (Frankfurt: Suhrkamp, 1979), abridged trans. Andrew Buchwalter, *Observations on "The Spiritual Situation of the Age": Contemporary German Perspectives* (Cambridge, Mass.: MIT Press, 1984).
4. Jürgen Habermas, *Erkenntnis und Interesse* (Frankfurt: Suhrkamp, 1968), trans. Jeremy J. Shapiro, *Knowledge and Human Interests* (Boston: Beacon, 1971), p. 314; Thomas McCarthy, *The Critical Theory of Jürgen Habermas,* (Cambridge, Mass.: MIT Press, 1978), p. 126.
5. Jürgen Habermas, *Autonomy and Solidarity: Interviews,* ed. Peter Dews (London: Verso, 1986), p. 74. These provide the clearest guide to Habermas' intellectual formation and public stands.
6. Ibid., pp. 77, 149–151.
7. Ibid., pp. 98, 150, 152, 192, 194; McCarthy, *Habermas,* p. 386.
8. Habermas, *Autonomy and Solidarity,* pp. 78, 98, 124, 153.
9. Ibid., pp. 47, 135, 145, 147, 216; Habermas, *Knowledge and Human Interests,* p. 288.
10. Colette Audry, "Socialism Tomorrow," in Miloš Nicolić, ed., *Socialism on the Threshhold of the Twenty-First Century* (London: Verso, 1985), p. 37. This was the tenth in a series of such conferences, which began in 1976; italics in original.
11. Pietro Ingrao, "The European Left and the Problems of a New Internationalism," in ibid., pp. 104–105.
12. Göran Therborn, "Leaving the Post Office Behind," in ibid., pp. 227, 246, 248, 250.
13. Erling Olsen, "The Dilemma of the Social-Democratic Labor Parties," *Daedalus,* 113 (Spring 1984): 193; "New Paths for Socialism," *The Economist,* Dec. 21, 1985.
14. Daniel Vernet, "Les métamorphoses du socialisme: V. Contremodèles du Nord et du Sud," *Le Monde,* Oct. 13, 1984.
15. Serge July, *Les années Mitterrand: Histoire baroque d'une normalisation inachevée* (Paris: Grasset, 1986), pp. 15, 19, 112–113, 175.
16. Philippe Bauchard, *La guerre des deux roses: Du rêve à la réalité, 1981–1985* (Paris: Grasset, 1986), p. 349.
17. July, *Années Mitterrand,* pp. 30, 38, 206. See also editor's introduction to George Ross et al., eds., *The Mitterrand Experiment* (Cambridge: Polity, 1987), p. 12.
18. For the text of The Yalta Memorandum, see Palmiro Togliatti, *On Gramsci and Other Writings,* trans. Derek Boothman (London: Lawrence and Wishart, 1979), p. 296.
19. Interview with Eugenio Scalfari, *La Repubblica* (Rome) Aug. 2, 1978.
20. Enrico Berlinguer et al., *After Poland: Towards a New Internationalism,*

trans. Antonio Bronda and Stephen Bodington (Nottingham: Spokesman, 1982), pp. 13–14, 30, 40, 42, 67.

21. Ingrao, "The European Left," p. 115.

nine. The Triad of the Greens

1. Otto Schily, "Le contre-pied de la tradition allemande," *Le Monde,* July 19, 1985.
2. Heinrich Böll, *Was soll aus dem Jungen bloss werden?* (Bornheim: Lamuv, 1981), trans. Leila Vennewitz, *What's To Become of the Boy?* (New York: Knopf, 1984), p. 4.
3. Anna Picardi-Montesardo, *Die Gastarbeiter in der Literatur der Bundesrepublik Deutschland* (Berlin: Express, 1985), p. 60.
4. Heinrich Böll, *Gruppenbild mit Dame* (Cologne: Kiepenheuer & Witsch, 1971), trans. Leila Vennewitz, *Group Portrait with Lady* (New York: McGraw Hill, 1973), p. 4.
5. I owe this formulation to my wife, Judith M. Hughes.
6. Gerd Langguth, *Der grüne Faktor: Von der Bewegung zur Partei?* (Zurich: Interfrom, 1984), trans. Richard Straus, *The Green Factor in German Politics: From Protest Movement to Political Party* (Boulder and London: Westview, 1985), p. 12; Emil-Peter Müller, *Die Grünen und das Parteiensystem* (Cologne: Deutscher Instituts-Verlag, 1984), p. 69.
7. Robert Gerald Livingston, "West Germany's Green Power," *Washington Quarterly,* 6 (Summer 1983): 179.
8. Müller, *Grünen und Parteiensystem,* p. 129.
9. On all the above, see the scrupulous and detailed analysis, ". . . und weiter sterben die Wälder," *Die Zeit,* 39 (Oct. 26, 1984).
10. Langguth, *Green Factor,* pp. 87–88.
11. Ibid., p. 90.
12. Jürgen Habermas, *Autonomy and Solidarity: Interviews,* ed. Peter Dews (London: Verso, 1986), p. 179.
13. Gunter Hofmann, "'Hier kann man nicht denken': Tagebuch einer Parlaments-Woche mit den Grünen," *Die Zeit,* 38 (May 20, 1983).
14. For the former, see *Programme of the German Green Party* (London: Heretic Books, 1983); for the latter, see the analyses in *Die Zeit,* 42 (Feb. 13, May 15, 1987).
15. Müller, *Grünen und Parteiensystem,* p. 155.

ten. Another Fin de Siècle?

1. Terry Eagleton in *The Times Literary Supplement,* Feb. 20, 1987.

2. Jürgen Habermas, *Autonomy and Solidarity: Interviews,* ed. Peter Dews (London: Verso, 1986), p. 178.

3. Jean-François Lyotard, *La Condition postmoderne: Rapport sur le savoir* (Paris: Minuit, 1979), trans. Geoff Bennington and Brian Massumi, *The Postmodern Condition: A Report on Knowledge* (Minneapolis: University of Minnesota Press, 1984), pp. 4–5.

4. As applied to Milan Kundera by François Ricard, "Satan's Point of View," trans. John Anzalone, *Salmagundi* (Winter 1987), p. 59.

5. Peter Glotz, "Forward to Europe," trans. John E. Woods, *Dissent* (Summer 1986), p. 335; italics in original.

6. Timothy Garton Ash, "Which Way Will Germany Go?" *The New York Review of Books,* 32 (Jan. 31, 1985).

7. For excerpts from Brandt's address, see "'Wir brauchen die Unbequemen,'" *Die Zeit,* 42 (June 26, 1987).

Index

167

168